Managing
Technological
Change

Managing Technological Change

A Strategic Partnership Approach

Carol Joyce Haddad
Eastern Michigan University

SAGE Publications
International Educational and Professional Publisher
Thousand Oaks ▪ London ▪ New Delhi

For information:

Sage Publications, Inc.
2455 Teller Road
Thousand Oaks, California 91320
E-mail: order@sagepub.com

Sage Publications Ltd.
6 Bonhill Street
London EC2A 4PU
United Kingdom

Sage Publications India Pvt. Ltd.
M-32 Market
Greater Kailash I
New Delhi 110 048 India

Printed in the United States of America

Library of Congress Cataloging-in-Publication Data

Haddad, Carol Joyce.
  Managing technological change : a strategic partnership approach / Carol Joyce Haddad.
      p. cm.
Includes bibliographical references and index.
  ISBN 0-7619-2563-5 (cloth) -- ISBN 0-7619-2564-3 (pbk.)
  1. Technological innovations--Management. 2. Organizational change--Management. 3. Technology--Management. I. Title.
  HD45 .H23 2002
  658.5'14--dc21

                                            2001007986

02 03 04 05 10 9 8 7 6 5 4 3 2 1

Acquiring Editor:	Marquita Flemming
Editorial Assistant:	MaryAnn Vail
Copy Editor:	Jonathan Preimesberger
Production Editor:	Claudia A. Hoffman
Indexer:	Molly Hall
Cover Designer:	Janet Foulger

Contents

Preface

The importance of managing the process of technological change is now well-recognized in theory and in practice. Organizations in all sectors of the economy have learned by trial and error that merely investing in new technology, without careful planning and ongoing assessment, does not necessarily result in improved business performance. As a result, the management of technology (MOT) has become a field of study in its own right—a hybrid grafted from the disciplines of engineering and business management.

Yet existing books on technology management are generally very applied and narrow in focus, emphasizing the research and development process, the engineering process, or the innovation process in general. Little is said about the organizational dimensions of technological change, and no mention is made of strategy-based partnerships with frontline technology users or their union representatives. Most of the existing technology management literature is also limited to the manufacturing sector. This book fills a critical void by presenting an integrative, strategic, and participative approach to technology management from a multi-industry perspective. This is accomplished by

- defining the concept of strategic partnership and presenting a rationale for its use;
- identifying the steps involved in successful technology planning, acquisition, development, implementation, and assessment;
- presenting an integrative framework that links aspects of systems theory, engineering design theory, adult education theory, and industrial relations theory to each of the aforementioned steps;
- discussing the barriers to rational innovation processes, using illustrative examples from service, public, and manufacturing sector industries; and
- offering illustrative examples of best practice from multiple industries and cross-national perspectives, especially those involving strategic partnerships.

The book combines theory with practice. It first presents interdisciplinary theoretical perspectives such as sociotechnical integration, dynamic systems, strategic innovation, user-centered design, and participative management models. These theories undergird the applied dimensions of this book, which offers practical guidelines for "good practice" technological change. Case study examples from industrial sectors, such as education, law enforcement, health care, and manufacturing, illustrate key concepts and approaches. A number of these case studies are based on my work as an action-researcher, consultant, and evaluator. Other cases have been conveyed to me by practitioners, some of whom have also been students in my graduate courses.

The organization of the book is as follows. Chapter 1 addresses how new workplace technology can improve performance—and how it can have the opposite effect when it is not properly planned and introduced with the participation of key stakeholders. Chapter 2 defines the concept of strategic partnership and, using illustrative examples, explains how it differs from simple labor-management cooperation and from strategic planning.

Chapter 3 presents an overview of the steps involved in technology planning, acquisition or development, implementation and assessment. The theoretical underpinnings of each of these steps come from systems theory, concurrent engineering, and industrial relations theory. Chapter 4 lists the elements of the needs assessment process and explains how technology and business goals factor into this process. It includes a discussion of cost justification procedures, as well as methods for determining an organization's "readiness for technological change."

Chapter 5 addresses ways of identifying and eliminating organizational barriers to technological change, such as organizational culture, poor labor relations, and employee feelings of disenfranchisement. Results of case study and survey research performed by the author in this area are provided. Chapter 6 offers a rationale for representative "design teams" and suggests methods for selection, operation, and interaction of such teams with the rest of the organization. It further outlines methods for implementing strategy-based change, using a partnership approach.

Chapter 7 discusses the importance of training and organizational learning to successful technology adoption and use. It offers practical guidance on training program design, draws from the theories of adult education, and highlights examples of successful training partnerships. Chapter 8 promotes the necessity for ongoing evaluation and monitoring to ensure that the technological change continues to meet organizational, business, and performance objectives. It also identifies ways of institutionalizing the strategic partnership approach to change.

I hope that managers, engineers, union representatives, and students will derive value from this work, and that it offers a unique contribution to the fields of technology and business management.

Acknowledgments

The students in my graduate courses in technology management at Eastern Michigan University have served over the years as sounding boards for the concepts presented herein. Six students—Karren Johnson, Paula Martin, Gladys Howard, Lance Williams, and Dorothy McAllen—contributed research material from which five of the case studies were based; Rick Pomorski alerted me to innovative technology acquisition practices in his workplace; and alumna and health care professional Carol Fletcher offered valuable feedback on the elements contained in Table 4.2. John Santomauro, director of the Canton Department of Public Safety, contributed an illustrative example of proactive needs assessment.

Eastern Michigan University provided me with a sabbatical leave, during which the majority of this book was written. I thank those colleagues who wrote letters in support of this competitively awarded leave—Paul Kuwik, Alphonso Bellamy, Denise Tanguay, and Timothy Doyle of Eastern Michigan University, Jeffrey Liker of the University of Michigan's Department of Industrial and Operations Engineering, and Ulrich Juergens of the Science Center Berlin for Social Research. I am also grateful to Robert Quinn of the University of Michigan Business School, whose endorsement of the book project at its inception served as a motivating vote of confidence.

A number of academics and practitioners were willing to serve as reviewers, offering valuable feedback on a draft of the manuscript. Special thanks is owed to Jeffrey Liker of the University of Michigan; William Cooke, director of the Fraser Center for Workplace Issues at Wayne State University; Richard Badham of the University of Wollongong; Narcyz Roztocki of the State University of New York New Paltz; Robert Brewster of Visteon Automotive Systems; and Rachel Apgar of Pilot Industries, Inc.

Throughout the writing process I was cheered on by loving family members and friends, in particular Margot I. Duley whose daily encouragement and intellectual mentoring were and are invaluable to my spirit and my psyche; George and Evelyn Haddad, George Haddad Jr., and Mary, Michael, and Alexander Raveane who have supported and encouraged this and all of my professional endeavors; and Joyce and Hy Kornbluh who provided steadfast support in the midst of Hy's terminal illness.

I am also indebted to Marquita Flemming of Sage Publications for her faith in this project and sound advice throughout the entire product life cycle, and to editorial staff members Claudia Hoffman, Jon Preimesberger, and all members of the Sage staff who played important roles in the book production process.

One

Technology's Perils and Promise

The Need for Technology Management

Investing in new technology is a costly venture. Before making such an investment, careful planning and selection should precede the purchase. Yet in today's fast-paced work environment, technology decisions do not always follow a well-conceived plan. When consumers buy new electronic devices such as televisions, they may spend some time reading specialty magazines that list features and consumer satisfaction ratings and then comparison shop for the best features and price. Alternatively, consumers may make impulsive purchases based on irrational criteria, such as the aesthetic appearance of the television set or the number of advertised features that they may never use.

Organizations, too, approach technology decision making in both rational and irrational ways. There may be an inclusive and focused planning process to select technologies for identified and feasible business goals. Alternatively, the glamour of technology, external challenges and competition, or internal political factors may play an influential role in the decision to adopt new equipment, integrated systems, and software. Even when planning occurs, the process may exclude key people who have valuable knowledge or information that can improve the implementation process and performance outcomes.

Technological Change:
Four Real-Life Scenarios

The following four case studies illustrate two very different patterns of planning and involvement. These real-life scenarios are from an elementary school, a public police agency, and two U.S.-based companies—an aircraft engine manufacturing plant belonging to a large, multi-industry company, and an automotive firm. In all cases, pseudonyms are used in place of the real company, plant, school, agency, union, and product names.

Learning Elementary School

A school district that was rapidly becoming a leader in the use of instructional technology, thanks to visionary leadership of the superintendent, an expanding and supportive populace, and the passage of funding bonds, sought to equip a newly constructed elementary school (which will be referred to here by the pseudonym "Learning") with state-of-the-art computer equipment. Anxious to outfit the new building before the start of classes and bypassing existing structures such as a technology-curriculum committee and the teachers' union, the superintendent and school principal decided to purchase 180 mobile laptop computers, which were arranged in groups of 36 on mobile carts that could be wheeled into classrooms as needed. Their thinking was that this would supplant the need for an additional computer lab (one large lab and a smaller one were included in the building design) and would permit more than one class to have computer access at the same time. The two administrators had attended a conference and made their equipment selection decisions based on what they had seen there.

The well-intentioned but nonetheless top-down decision-making process led to a "disastrous start" in the words of one district official. The laptops were low-end machines and were purchased without wireless cards. Wires had to be attached to each of the machines, creating a tripping hazard. Teachers had to move the carts and make sure the equipment was operational before the start of each class and return the carts at the conclusion of the class period. The machines lacked floppy disk drives, and students had to save their work to the network rather than to disk, thereby prohibiting them from doing additional work on class projects at the library or at home. The small laptop screens had poor resolution, and frequent breakdowns of the equipment caused a loss of teacher and student confidence in the computers.

Many teachers shunned the laptops, and some declared that a second computer lab would have better met their needs. In the end, the school had to equip the laptops with wireless cards. This upgrade raised the investment per machine to a level that was comparable to higher-end laptops or desktops. Even with the upgrade, breakdowns continued to occur past the warranty period. The original decision to purchase these machines was made more expeditiously than a committee decision might have been. But the machines that were selected did not meet teacher or student needs and were not cost-effective. Because of the poor reputation that followed them in the school, they also served as a disincentive to teachers who were already reluctant to use computers in their teaching.

Community Police

A community police agency (referred to here by the pseudonym "Community Police") with large geographic coverage sought a more efficient way of dispatching cars in response to calls for assistance. The system the police had been using consisted of a dispatcher who received the telephone call, dispatched a patrol car, and then completed an incident report that was filed in a storage area. This method had two perceived shortcomings: There was no link to information already on file about previous incidents at the same address, and the closest car was not always the one that was dispatched.

The chief of police attended a conference at which computer-aided dispatch (CAD) systems were discussed. This technology would electronically log each incoming call and, using a caller identification system, would display any information on file about previous incidents involving the caller or address. The dispatcher would add information collected during the conversation and dispatch a police officer to the site. After responding to the situation, the officer would call the dispatcher and verify information received. All of this information was then to be housed in the CAD system's storage-and-retrieval database. After speaking with top-level managers from other police agencies, the chief of police decided to adopt a CAD system at Community Police.

The decisions surrounding the adoption and implementation of the CAD system were made in a top-down manner. The agency's information technology (IT) department developed technical specifications for the new system, selected the CAD vendor, and coordinated the implementation process. None of the dispatchers, patrol officers, or lower-level managers were consulted, nor were the unions representing the police officers and dispatchers or the director of human resources. Although minimal training of dispatchers was planned using a "train-the-trainer" model, no training was offered because the dispatchers' union objected to them taking on this extra responsibility without compensation, which the agency would not pay. The delegation of implementation duties to the IT department also meant that there was no executive-level manager overseeing the process.

The lack of user involvement and training led to ineffective use of the new CAD system. Dispatchers did not fully understand how its storage-and-retrieval feature worked and consequently kept information in a temporary storage area instead of transferring it to the permanent database where it could be recalled by the computer for future incidents. The vendor, after learning that only 10% of the system's capability was being used, concluded that the agency was wasting money and resources. Dispatchers and their supervisors were ambivalent about the new system and felt no sense of ownership or comprehension of its capabilities. Another inefficiency was the lack of interface of the new system with the radio system used by patrol officers. In short, the agency did not reap the intended efficiency benefits of the new system, despite a significant expenditure of funds and effort.

The Brownvale Story

The Brownvale plant of the Heavy Industry Corporation (HIC) manufactured and tested large turbine engines used in commercial and military aircraft (both "Brownvale" and "HIC" are pseudonyms). With a workforce of 17,000, the plant had been in continuous operation since the late 1940s, with different unions representing production and maintenance/ trades employees. Labor-management relations were somewhat poor, especially with the production employee union. Engines were produced under contract for government and commercial customers in the United States and 48 foreign nations. The aircraft engine group to which Brownvale belonged was one of 20 product groups within HIC, accounting for nearly 20% of the parent corporation's income. Heightened demand for aircraft engines, particularly military aircraft engines purchased by the Pentagon, had caused production volume at the plant to expand from 300 to 1,150 engines in a 3-year period.

Despite increased product demand, the company sought to trim operating costs to maintain industry competitiveness and position itself to withstand termination of certain engine programs. Improving the efficiency of operations through new technology and eventual workforce reductions was the strategy guiding the change process. Central to this efficiency goal was the introduction of a computer-controlled parts storage and retrieval system known as the automated storage and retrieval system (ASRS). Storing parts remotely would increase the floor space available for assembly work, thereby enabling the plant to more quickly meet product demand without a building expansion.

The Technological Change

The ASRS was to consist of four subsystems: (a) a section of the assembly building known as the receiving, input, and dispatch (RID) area where incoming parts were inspected, identified, sorted, labeled, and scanned before being transported to assembly or storage; (b) a separate building known as the central storage unit (CSU) containing a storage system using 85-foot-high storage bins and computer-controlled cranes for large parts storage and 5,400 drawers for the storage of small parts; (c) "kitting" stations, at which engine parts along with the precise accessories needed for each part were to have been combined into "kits" before being sent to the assembly conveyors; and (d) transfer cars and automated guided vehicles (AGVs) to deliver parts from storage to assembly "just-in-time."

Technology Decision Making

The plan for the ASRS was developed by two high-level managers representing assembly expansion and planning and assembly operations, based on a study performed by an external consultant. They drew up specifications for a new system and solicited bids from engineering firms for the design and installation. The contract engineer who designed the RID portion of the ASRS and who drew up the implementation plan for the CSU was ultimately hired as the unit manager for hourly employees at the Brownvale engine plant.

Although a few high-ranking managers from the assembly area were drawn into the decision-making process after the idea for the Central Storage Unit was conceived and approved, involvement of lower-level managers and hourly employees was not solicited until after construction of the CSU was under way. At that point, the newly hired unit manager created two implementation teams for the CSU: (a) a Technology Transition Team consisting of salaried employees; and (b) a User Involvement Team consisting of hourly employees from all three shifts. The purpose of these teams, on which members served on a voluntary basis, was to provide forums for communication, user involvement, training ideas, and implementation planning. The User Involvement Team also served as the start-up user group. Both teams were disbanded within the first month that the ASRS came online.

The company met with representatives of the maintenance and trades union (MTU) to comply with an advance notification of technology requirement contained in the collective bargaining agreement, but management had already made decisions about technology design and installation.

Impact on Job Content

The ASRS required considerable job restructuring and new learning on the part of operators who had to use it. Instead of placing logged parts in storage bins by hand, movement of parts was now accomplished with conveyors, cranes, and other equipment, controlled with a new VAX computer system. Location and retrieval of improperly stored parts from an 80-foot-high unit was far more difficult than it had been under the hand storage system. Despite the added complexity and responsibility of the operators' work, there was no upgrading of their classification or salary rate.

Maintenance and trades employees fared better under the new system. They worked alongside company and equipment vendor representatives to install the CSU technology, receiving coveted overtime pay during the setup and "debugging" phases. Still, despite their vital role in system maintenance and repair, there was no upgrading of job classification or pay, even with the urging of their union. Instead, the company created a new repair position, rated three steps below the unionized maintenance and repair classification, and filled the jobs with new hires.

The ASRS affected managers differentially by rank. Those centrally involved in technology decision making (typically unit managers and above) described the technology in positive terms. Lower-level managers and supervisors responsible for the smooth operation of the CSU confessed that problems with the system software caused them grief and that some components of the ASRS might be abandoned.

Job Training

Training plans for all hourly and salaried employees working with the CSU were drawn up while the system was still in the design and development phase. Managers attended meetings and received an implementation plan manual with detailed information about system design and intended operation. Methods engineers had been given manuals prepared by the in-plant Learning Center on how to design parts kits, and systems analysts, systems programmers, and computer programmers were sent to the software engineering firm for 5 months to participate in and learn the CSU programming. Maintenance and trades employees were given some classroom and on-the-job training by the software vendor, but contrary to the plan, no technical employee was provided by the engineering firm to work with maintenance staff in a troubleshooting capacity.

The training program for operators in the CSU was particularly detailed and well-planned. The company's Learning Center hired a trainer more than a year before system start-up to work exclusively with CSU hourly employees on a temporary but full-time basis. The trainer developed a comprehensive training manual that described through photographs, pictures, and text the functions and proper use of each of the pieces of equipment in the automated storage and retrieval system. The training plan was to have consisted of two parts: (a) first classroom training outlining the system's function and operation; and (b) then "hands-on" training of individuals at each of the workstations to cross-train them for later job rotation to accommodate production needs.

However, this training plan was abandoned in the face of uneven implementation of the ASRS because of software problems and the push to bring it online before they were resolved. Operators were required to work with the system without hands-on training; the vendor ultimately offered some training during system testing while operations were running.

Classroom training was offered to production workers, but the trainer complained that technical managers consistently failed to inform her of changes in the software, despite repeated requests for information on system updates. This resulted in frustration for both the trainer and the operators using the computer terminals. Moreover, training focused on the rote sequence of job tasks without adequate explanation of the workings of the entire system. For example, operators were expected to type into the computers numeric codes linked to specific storage locations, without having the meaning of the codes explained to them.

Implementation and Outcomes

The desire to clear assembly floor space placed pressure on CSU managers to implement the system before it had been adequately tested. As one manager noted: "When you're doing development and production simultaneously, you run into trouble. . . . it's been a long, painful year as a result of all those things." An operator stated the problems facing management more bluntly: "The supervisors don't know any more about operating the system than the workers."

There was also tension between operators and salaried technical employees involved with the CSU. Employees using the VAX computers complained that they were denied access to certain computer screens and menus, thus restricting their ability to solve problems as they arose. These workers further complained of stress arising from frequent malfunction of the storage and retrieval system. This also placed pressure on the assemblers who often did not receive needed parts in time. Fear of job elimination was an added source of worry.

The division of labor involved in programming the software for the CSF system appeared to have placed pressures on technical employees as well. The operating systems for the computers themselves were written by the computer manufacturer. Applications programs were written by an external engineering firm located in another state, and technical employees from the plant were sent to that firm for 5 months to learn the programming so that it could be adapted to specific company needs. However, when problems emerged with the new system, the burden of correcting them fell primarily on the technicians in the Brownvale plant. Software problems were compounded by the self-imposed isolation of technicians from production workers, who were not consulted when problems arose. Problems persisted with the ASRS for months after the system went online.

Two ASRS subsystems were scrapped before becoming fully operational. One subsystem, involved in the placing of small parts in kits for assembly, had been plagued with software problems from the start and was not operational months after the ASRS went online. The AGV's subsystem also proved to be short-lived. After investing $3 million on the installation of imbedded wire track and equipment, management questioned the feasibility of using the track system to deliver parts to 800 separate workstations and developed a modified plan to transfer parts to "drop points" located throughout the assembly area.

Technical malfunctions were compounded by poor labor relations. The popular unit manager, who had tried to include union-represented production employees in the implementation process, and one of his supervisors were replaced in a move widely referred to in the plant as the "Saturday Night Massacre." Management described this action as normal internal reshuffling, but a production union representative speculated that the company thought the unit manager had gone too far in his employee involvement in technology implementation efforts.

In the end, although the ASRS worked eventually, management decisions concerning its adoption and implementation adversely affected performance of the system and the attitudes of operators and even of supervisors and trainers toward it.

The Amcar Corporation

The U.S.-based Amcar Corporation (pseudonym for an automobile manufacturer), faced with declining market share and long lead times for new product development, undertook a bold restructuring of its engineering, business, and manufacturing operations. The existing system of sequential development by component experts operating within functional groups was replaced by product-focused, cross-functional teams guided by a concurrent engineering philosophy. These teams, which averaged roughly 500 to 700 people, were divided into smaller teams focused on a general aspect of the vehicle, such as interior engineering, and further subdivided into departments of 12 to 40 people on the basis of specific components such as seats and restraints (Haddad, 1996a). Flexible groups could form to solve specific problems as needed. The overriding motivation for this structural change was cutting Amcar's 6-year product development time in half while containing costs and improving quality.

Plant-Level Labor-Management Cooperation

The first car to be fully developed under this new structure was a subcompact called "Flash." Encouraged by Amcar's selection of their plant as the build site for this vehicle, plant management and the local union representing production and maintenance employees developed a cooperative partnership. They negotiated a "progressive operating agreement" that provided a joint framework for voluntary employee involvement in activities such as continuous quality improvement, self-directed work groups, job rotation, ergonomic improvement, and an employee-administered performance recognition program. The plant manager and local union president cochaired weekly quality meetings, and the union bargaining committee was invited to weekly meetings with plant management to discuss shop floor concerns such as health and safety, work schedules, and work process. Also, for the first time, the local union president and shop chairman were invited alongside the plant manager to meetings with each of the suppliers, to identify and resolve potential design and manufacturability problems.

Employee Input in Product Design

One significant change from past Amcar practice was the engineering group's solicitation of early input from manufacturing plant hourly employees. Assemblers were invited to the technical center 150 weeks before product launch to offer ergonomic and manufacturability input on vehicle and component concept design. This was a significant departure from the customary delay of their involvement until the pilot-build activity—22 weeks before launch.

Assemblers also played a more active role in the first prototype build, which occurred 95 weeks before launch. Two to three assemblers called "production specialists" voluntarily served on component-focused launch teams of 10 to 15 employees alongside representatives from each of the functional groups serving on the platform team (e.g., design and process engineers, procurement and supply personnel), and technical staff from supplier firms. Decisions were made by consensus, so every team member had to be satisfied with the result before moving on to the next item. Never before had assemblers had what amounted to veto power over upstream technology and ergonomic decisions pertaining to the equipment and processes to be used at individual workstations.

To participate on the product launch teams, assemblers were required to travel to Amcar's technical center for 2 weeks at a time on a rotating basis. Although they did not receive extra pay for their participation, they welcomed the opportunity to earn a salary during what would normally be layoff for model changeover. Back at their home plant, assemblers offered classroom training to prepare fellow workers for the pilot build. The learning was reciprocal, for assembly and maintenance employees engaged in "inspection tear downs" of prototype vehicles offered valuable suggestions for the pilot build.

In all, 50% of the unionized assembly and maintenance employees participated as team members in process verification decisions at Amcar's technical center. They also worked at tooling firms to assist with the building of tools and equipment and the testing of trial parts for process integrity. On occasion, engineers even telephoned assemblers after hours for advice on the resolution of design problems. Also for the first time in Amcar's history, pilot-build vehicles were loaned to hourly assemblers for test driving.

Months after product launch, process teams still operated with plant assemblers and process engineers to resolve manufacturing problems. It was reported in a national union magazine that the company used more than half of the 4,000 suggestions offered by production and maintenance employees throughout the product development and manufacturing periods, which reinforced the belief that the company was serious about employee input.

Performance Outcomes

Amcar gained from the early involvement of assembly and maintenance employees in the product-process design. Tangible, measurable benefits included a reduction of product development time to 31 months— 3 weeks ahead of schedule and a full year sooner than the lead time for earlier passenger vehicles. The second key benefit was lower cost, for the Flash program was two thirds of the cost of comparable subcompact development at domestic competitors. According to one corporate executive, a significant portion of this saving was due to the early involvement of plant employees, thereby avoiding costly engineering changes late in the process (Haddad, 2000a).

A less tangible but equally important benefit was the breaking down of discipline-based and hierarchical boundaries, and the sharing of information within cross-functional teams. This approach created a climate of organizational learning that continued long after product launch. It also reversed decades of mutual prejudices that engineers and assemblers held about each other. For the first time, each group spoke favorably about the contributions of the other in the development of the new car. One measurable indication of this organizational climate change was the sharp reduction in the number of grievances—from 4,000 per year to 50 during the 12 months before product launch. Unfortunately, these positive changes did not endure the changing of plant managers following the launch of the Flash.

Lessons Learned

These case studies present contrasting pictures of technology development and implementation strategies. Although the changes in each organization were strategy-driven, the top-down, nonparticipative methods used at Learning Elementary School, Community Police, and the Brownvale plant led to adoption of technologies that in some cases were not best suited to the operation, and in all cases wasted money, caused technology start-up problems, and adversely affected employee attitudes toward the new technology.

For example, Brownvale plant management did not involve frontline workers, the unions, or even supervisors in decisions about how to design or implement the new ASRS. The manager of the CSU, an engineer hired from the consulting firm that designed the system, did include production and maintenance employees as members of an implementation team, but his tenure as head of that unit was short-lived.

Training at Brownvale was offered after system installation and start-up, and production employees felt the stress of trying to learn to use a new system while fully engaged in parts storage and retrieval operations. The trainer felt that classroom training should have been offered before system start-up, using problem-solving exercises that simulated likely shop floor scenarios. Following classroom training with hands-on training on a fully operational and debugged system might have reduced system malfunctions and employee frustration.

Rigid divisions of labor exacerbated and even caused problems with the system. Software programmers and systems technicians saw no need to share details about program changes with the trainer or with production employees. Maintenance and trades employees were not called upon to provide feedback to the programmers and technicians following system repairs. Higher-level managers did not routinely share information about strategy and overall design with unit supervisors and managers. These divisions based on job function and organizational hierarchy that preceded the introduction of the technology persisted well after its adoption.

By the time the implementation of the new system was complete, employee confidence in it had faltered. This was true even among supervisory employees, who had full responsibility for ensuring that parts were correctly logged and stored but who played no significant role in the needs analysis for or design of the storage and retrieval plan. Brownvale is a story of opportunity lost, for the rocky adoption scenario that unfolded might have been avoided by focusing attention on the organizational requirements of the technological system, and by planning the change in partnership with employees and their unions.

In contrast, the Amcar Corporation illustrates *some* dimensions of a successful strategic partnership change effort. Although strategy was developed at the top of the organizational pyramid and pushed downward, the organizational restructuring that was imposed created opportunities for reaching across the great divides of discipline and task, resulting in synergistic development of new technological product and methods. The door that was opened for hourly worker involvement in the process was held open for local union leadership as well. The result was an atmosphere in which past grievances were put aside to work for the greater good of developing a new product that all could be proud of. Employees felt that for once their input was valued—and indeed it was. The partnership did not fully extend outward to embrace corporate management and the national union, and the lack of such a strategic alliance caused the Flash plant to become a victim of its own success when the popular plant manager was transferred elsewhere to guide the launch of another new vehicle.

The Amcar example illustrates the benefits of upstream involvement of key organizational stakeholders, and the fragility of partnerships when they are not cultivated from the highest levels of each stakeholder group. Who are the stakeholders? Stakeholders are defined groups that have a direct interest in the organization's activities and that are formally linked by virtue of structure or institutional/external power. It is quite common for organizations to recognize external stakeholders such as customers,

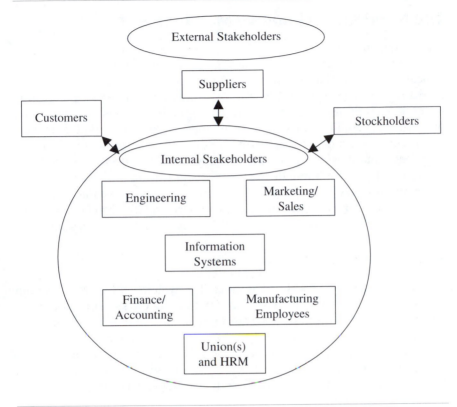

Figure 1.1   Representation of a Manufacturing Company's Key Stakeholders

suppliers, and stockholders or taxpayers. Yet *internal* constituents are also important stakeholders. Included in this category are representatives of functional groups such as design engineering, marketing and sales, finance, information systems, process engineering, manufacturing plant representatives—both salaried and hourly workers and the union(s) representing them—and the human resource managers.

Figure 1.1 depicts stakeholder groups for a manufacturing company. In a different sector, some of these categories would change. For example, in an elementary public school, parents, community representatives, and school board representatives would be external stakeholders, and curriculum experts, library and media specialists, teachers, the principal and other administrators, and teacher union representatives would be internal stakeholders.

The Need for Technology Management

The management of technological change is not an ideal but, rather, a necessity. As the Learning Elementary, Community Police, Brownvale, and Amcar cases illustrate, performance outcomes depend on the decisions made at each step of the design and implementation processes. Investing in new technology—no matter how sophisticated—is no assurance of improved quality, efficiency, or responsiveness to market demands. A growing awareness of this fact has caused the management of technology (MOT) to blossom as a field of study. MOT has been described as a marriage of two traditional disciplines—engineering and business management (Badawy, 1988). When the subfields of sociotechnical systems theory, engineering design theory, and industrial relations theory are taken into account, MOT can be viewed as an interdisciplinary area of study.

Systems Integration

A central tenet of MOT is the need for systems *integration*. Gaynor (1996) encourages thinking of MOT as "managing the system" and "managing the pieces" through integration of interdependent technological and organizational components (p. 1.5). This means that all vital research, engineering and technical, and business groups within an organization—including the human resource management function—must work together to design, plan, implement, and evaluate technological change.

The Nature of Technology

Technology includes the "hardware" of tools, equipment, machinery, and integrated systems such as the automated storage and retrieval system, and the "software" of computer programming that enables these systems to run. Researchers have developed useful typologies for categorizing technology by "level of mechanization" according to the degree of operator control or self-regulation (Bright, 1958; Butera & Thurman, 1984), or by its material transformation capability (Blackburn, Coombs, & Green, 1985). However, it is limiting to think of technology as only hardware and software.

Technology also refers to *knowledge*—the knowledge of inventing, designing, developing, operating, applying, maintaining, and repairing the hardware and software. A category of knowledge is *technique*—the skill-based method of using tools, machines, and software (Braun, 1998). This involves the ability to "exercise mental judgment" in the determination of work tasks based on available information (Jacques, 1961, as cited in Blauner, 1964). Technique also relies on "tacit skill"—subjective determinations involving "feel" and "discretion" (Manwaring & Wood, 1984; Zuboff, 1988).

The Nature of Management

Understanding the theory of technology management necessitates examining the term "*management*." Management refers to organizational structures, rules, and processes for decision making and direction in the attainment of performance outcomes. Subsystems include the human resource management function, the industrial relations system, the communication system, and the informal processes, and relationships that support and, at times, contradict formal governance procedures. Management is meant to drive and coordinate how things get done.

Philosophies of management play a major role in shaping organizational structures, levels of authority, reporting relationships, and degree of institutional control. One of the most influential and persistent management philosophies used to bridge the disciplines of engineering and management was put forward in the late 19th and early 20th centuries by an engineer named Frederick Winslow Taylor. Dubbed "scientific management," it was a system intent on identifying the "best" and most efficient way of performing each task and job through elaborate time-and-motion studies of production and craft workers.

Four principles served as the heart of this philosophy:

1. development and codification of a standardized way of performing job tasks to replace workers' "rule-of-thumb" methods;

2. "scientific" selection and training of workers;

3. management cooperation with the workers to ensure that work was performed according to the "scientific" principles developed; and

4. equal division of work and responsibility for work between management and workers, with management taking over "all work for which they are better fitted than the workmen" (Taylor, 1911, p. 3).

Taylor clarified this latter point by stating that "rules, laws and formulae" should "replace the judgement of the individual workman" thereby freeing him up to perform the physical tasks in the most efficient manner (Taylor, 1911, p. 4).

This attempted removal of the planning process from the execution of job tasks stemmed from Taylor's belief that workers lacked the necessary "education" or "mental capacity" to understand the scientific principles to be followed "without the aid of a man better educated than he is" (Taylor, 1911, p. 5). A piece-rate pay system was to serve as the incentive for workers succumbing to having their work timed by stopwatch and giving up all discretion about how to perform tasks.

Scientific management was questioned and bitterly resisted in its day, particularly by skilled craft workers (Kanigel, 1997; Montgomery, 1979;

Penn, 1982); and modern writers have concluded that "it never was a science, but rather a control system" (Thompson & McHugh, 1990, p. 64). Howard Rosenbrock (1990), himself an emeritus professor of control engineering, argues that Taylor "mined a rich seam of fantasy" (p. 134) and that his use of the word *science* was a term "of art" rather than fact (p. 138). Rosenbrock also takes Taylor to task for failing to credit Charles Babbage for the ideas seemingly borrowed from him, and for equating a production system with a causal machine.

Notwithstanding this criticism, Taylor's popularity with and impact on the field of industrial engineering has been substantial. The principles set forth in his 1911 book were delivered before assembled members of the American Society of Mechanical Engineers (ASME), an organization that had chosen him as its president in 1906. Thereafter, schools of engineering developed curricula in "efficiency engineering" (Pursell, 1995).

Taylor's principles remain popular in some circles, particularly as a justification for certain efficiencies in "lean production" operations (Adler, 1993). Yet even where work teams have some discretion in setting production standards, upstream design and engineering dictates place limits on their procedural discretion, as does the expectation that work teams be occupied nearly every second of a working minute. As Jürgens, Malsch, and Dohse (1993) have observed, "Toyotism" as they call the Japanese lean production system, with its "zero buffer and zero-error objectives" has "negative implications from the point of view of the employees and society" (p. 51).

In fact, the notion that the planning and design of work should be performed by trained engineers and managers and separated from the execution of work by production and trades employees is quite the opposite of concurrent engineering (Haddad, 1994). In its broadest application, this latter philosophy is an attempt to reduce downstream engineering and manufacturing problems by involving assembly and maintenance employees in upstream design decisions, as was done in the Amcar example. Scientific management is also the opposite of the philosophy espoused in this book—that of strategic, integrative, and participative technology management. The next chapter sets forward a definition of just what this philosophy entails.

The Value of Technology Management

Effective management of the technological change process is premised on a sound business strategy, planned in partnership with major stakeholders, and designed to be synergistic with organizational structures and functions. The principles put forward throughout this volume go beyond traditional MOT theory by viewing employees and union representatives as central players in technology planning and implementation.

Summary

Some organizations use planned and participative methods when adopting new technology, whereas in others decisions are made in piece-meal fashion based on short-term needs. The Learning Elementary, Community Police, and Brownvale case studies on the one hand, and the Amcar example on the other, illustrate these two contrasting approaches. At the Brownvale plant, the company introduced an ASRS to increase assembly floor space and enable the company to better meet product demand. The decision-making process for the technology selection was top-down, and the push to use the new system before it was fully tested and without adequate training of employees caused multiple problems. Technology selection at Learning Elementary and Community Police was also made in a top-down manner and did not yield the intended instructional performance results until costly modifications were made. In contrast, the Amcar case illustrates some dimensions of a strategic partnership approach by involving employees and their union representatives in the design and launch of a new product, resulting in an dramatic shortening of the development process and other tangible benefits.

Cases such as Brownvale, Community Police, and Learning Elementary have caused a broader recognition of the need for the systematic management of technological change (MOT) and for the emergence of a field of study devoted to its theory and practice. Technology refers not only to tools, equipment, and software but also to the knowledge involved in the invention, design, development, use, and maintenance of those items. The term "management" refers to theories such as "scientific management," as well as to structures, rules, and processes for decision making and direction to attain performance outcomes. Scientific management, which presumes that the planning of work should be performed by engineering and managerial experts and separated from the execution of tasks, is the antithesis of the philosophy advocated in this book—one of strategic, integrative, and participative change.

Two

Strategic Partnership

A Working Definition

To reap the greatest benefit from new technology, organizations must strategically plan the process of change. Surprisingly, technology investment is often devoid of strategy. Simply having a goal without a complete road map for attaining it does not constitute strategy. Take the hypothetical example of a school district's plan to provide new laptop computers to every teacher who requests one, along with home Internet access, provided that the teacher attends an approved training course. The district's goal is to encourage teachers to become familiar with computers during their personal time, in the hope that educators will more readily use computers for classroom instruction, class administration, and electronic communication with students and parents. If the district plan focuses only on the method by which computer models and vendors are to be selected, it is missing important components. Other issues to include in the plan are evaluating in advance the quality and appropriateness of the training courses, providing teachers with in-school resources to assist them in developing computer-based lesson plans, supplying extra computers to schools for student use, and reducing class size so that teachers can be available to individual students online as well as in the classroom.

Preece (1995), among others, implores managers to have a strategy for technology adoption. He offers a number of reasons to support this claim: the high expense of technology adoption; its potential to provide the organization with a competitive advantage through improved productivity, management, performance, and new lines of business; its revolutionary effect on management information system; and its effect on the organization and its many stakeholders (p. 15). Preece is quick to point out the "integrative potential" of new technology insofar as it enables linkage across functional departments and with external constituents such as customers and suppliers (p. 16). Yet, although many organizations engage in some level of planning, they lack an explicit technology strategy (Preece, 1995, p. 23).

Strategic Technology Planning

Definition and First Steps

Strategic technology planning is the process of developing a goal-oriented, step-by-step procedure for technology selection or development, adoption, and use. Although in theory such a plan will follow a rational systems model, it should include processes for dealing with contingencies and for creativity (Brown & Eisenhardt, 1998; Mintzberg, 1994). The technology strategy must be in alignment with and support the organization's mission, priorities, and strategic business objectives.

The need to align technology strategy with business strategy cannot be assumed or overstated. Both strategies must work in tandem to ensure optimal organizational performance and the delivery of high-quality products or service to the marketplace and to society at-large. Cleland and Bursic (1992) pose five useful questions that can serve as the first steps in business and technology strategy integration:

1. What mix of products [services] and markets is required to meet the financial [and strategic] objectives of the firm or organization?
2. What supporting processes are required to be successful in those products [services] and markets?
3. What technologies are required to develop the products and processes?
4. What investments are required to develop and integrate business and technological objectives?
5. How will this information compare with the competition's strategies? (pp. 38–39)

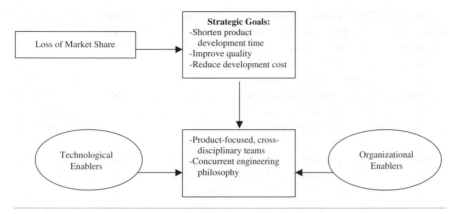

Figure 2.1   Amcar's Technology and Business Strategy Integration

Amcar Example

Amcar (pseudonym for an automotive firm discussed in Chapter 1) provided a good example of how business strategy drove the process of change, and how technological and organizational innovation interacted to support business goals. Spurred by a loss of market share, Amcar recognized a need to shorten product development time while improving product quality and lowering the cost of the process. The company reorganized its engineering and business functional operations into product-focused, cross-disciplinary teams (see Figure 2.1). These large teams of 500 to 700 people were divided into smaller teams, departments, and problem-solving groups that focused on particular vehicle components.

Technology was used to facilitate intra- and intergroup communication. First, the company built a new, 3-million-square-foot facility to house design, vehicle engineering, pilot assembly, and training activities under one roof for the first time ever. The building was designed to allow colocation of teams, with each vehicle team inhabiting an entire floor. Functional groups (e.g., instrument panel product engineers) working on one vehicle were located directly above or below their counterparts on another vehicle team. On each floor, managers' officers lined atrium corridors, were visible through glass walls, and were adjacent to a large open room housing work cubicles of staff engineers and designers. Each floor had a multitude of conference rooms and an education center.

A second technological enabler of the business strategy was widespread use of information and communication technologies. A new computer-aided design (CAD) system permitted designers and engineers to create 3-dimensional solid figures instead of relying on 2-dimensional blueprints as in the past. Most important, the CAD system was available electronically—via desktop computer—to all members of a design team, including suppliers. CAD images could also be projected onto a conference room screen, enabling team members to solve engineering problems collectively, in real time. A corporate-wide local area network (LAN) and an electronic mail system supplemented the telephone and walks to colleagues' workstations as vehicles for intra- and intergroup communication.

A number of organizational enablers also supported the cross-functional team operation, including reduced levels of managerial hierarchy, staff engineer empowerment in decision making, scheduled meetings of technical specialists across platform teams, a performance appraisal system that rewarded teamwork and lower-level decision making, a training matrix to support learning and skill acquisition, cross-functional job mobility, and career ladders that allowed salaried employees to advance in either technical or managerial tracks.

Technology's Strategic Advantage

Cleland and Bursic (1992) point out that the traditional technology management approach has been to fit technology strategy into business strategy, without paying adequate attention to the fact that technology investment or development can also bring new business opportunities to the organization (p. 39). This can be illustrated by a university's investment in the expertise needed to place some of its courses on the World Wide Web. This enables the school to attract nontraditional adult learners, distance students, and others who cannot or prefer not to attend classes on campus. It also permits the university to develop international, cross-cultural components for its programs without necessarily requiring overseas travel.

Strategic Planning Steps

Strategic business planning should precede decisions about technology development or acquisition. The first step in strategic planning, as is depicted in Figure 2.2, is generally an internal and external environmental scan. Benchmarking is one such externally focused method in which a company's, agency's, or institution's internal structures and operations, market practices, products, and services are compared to those of one or more competitors. Another such method, Delphi forecasting, involves interviewing a panel of experts to predict certain business, product, or service trends.

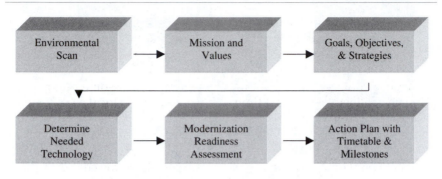

Figure 2.2   Strategic Planning Process Model

A popular method for conducting an environmental scan is to examine the strengths, challenges or weaknesses, opportunities, and threats facing an organization. This exercise is popularly referred to as a SCOT (strengths, challenges, opportunities, threats) or SWOT (strengths, weaknesses, opportunities, threats) analysis. Assessment of current and potential products or services, markets and customers, technology and infrastructure, financial resources, human resources, organizational and management structures, and core competencies should be built into each level of analysis. A SCOT analysis is best when performed by the representatives of a broadest possible cross section of internal stakeholder groups. Table 2.1 presents an abbreviated example of what a SCOT analysis for a fictitious medium-size public university might look like.

The second major step in strategic planning is to develop or revise the organization's mission statement. This statement is an articulation of how the business, agency, or educational institution views itself, and what it aspires to be. Institutional values play a role in the formulation of the mission. Large or strategically significant divisions or departments within an organization often have their own mission statements as well as those of the entire company, agency, or institution. For example, the mission statement of the information systems (IS) department of a large health insurance provider (which will be referred to here by the pseudonym "Good Health") is as follows:

> The mission of the Good Health Information Services family is to provide, through our personal commitment to excellence, best-in-class technology systems services and products by exceeding customer expectations through the delivery capabilities of our team of empowered IS professionals. Compassion for one another, open communication, teamwork, and job satisfaction will produce customer satisfaction, value for price paid, and outstanding business results.

Table 2.1 Example of a SCOT Analysis for a Medium-Size Public University

	Strengths	Challenges	Opportunities	Threats
Products/ Services	- Courses taught by knowledgeable faculty who perform research - State-of-the-art library	- Faculty morale in need of improvement because of lagging salaries - Underfunded student services	- Expand online/ off-campus course offerings for targeted markets - Specialized student services	- Attrition of student population before graduation - Public impatience with time to graduation
Customers/ Markets	- Diverse student body (women, minorities, & international) - Nearby employers with tuition assistance	- Many students work full time - Stiff competition from other nearby and distance colleges	- Aging nearby population - Coworkers of alumni - Continuing education for employees in many sectors	- Competition from "online" university - Students prefer schools with better facilities & services
Technology/ Infrastructure	- On and off-campus access to library periodicals via Internet - Some modernized buildings - Compact campus	- Some faculty offices lack powerful computers - Cumbersome online student record system - Aging buildings	- Corporate donations of used machines - State-of-art classrooms to support innovative programs	- Inability to quickly renovate & equip main classroom buildings - Commuters want convenient parking
Financial resources	- Recent appropriations for building construction - Balanced budget	- Lower state appropriation - Reputation for low tuition	- Increase alumni/ business contributions - Increase grants - Lobby state	- Expected budget shortfall - Larger class sizes will thwart quality

(Continued)

Table 2.1 (Continued)

	Strengths	*Challenges*	*Opportunities*	*Threats*
Human resources	- Majority of faculty are full-time	- Older, more costly faculty	- Offer early retirement incentives	- Loss of staff & faculty to better-funded employers
Organizational structure	- Departments organized by functional specialization	- Limited cross-departmental teaching	- Programs such as Women's Studies involve many departments	- Departments competing for scarce funds
Management structure	- Faculty governance structures - Leadership invested in president & regents	- Partisan appointment of regents - Faculty/staff lack strong input in selection of top officers	- Faculty & staff willingness to serve on improvement committees	- Senior administrators insulated from staff, faculty, & students
Core competencies	- Education of K-12 teachers - Strong liberal & fine arts - Ability to respond quickly to market needs	- Some programs not distinct enough from those at competitor schools	- Better marketing of core programs through multimedia sources & alumni	- State funding cuts and possible recession limit resources for core programs

Terms such as "best-in-class" or "world class," "commitment to excellence," and "customer satisfaction" are quite typical of mission statements.

Goals emanate from the mission statement. Here are the goals, in this case referred to as the vision statement, for the Good Health company's IS department:

- To be a world-class IS organization
- To exceed customer expectations
- To offer consultation, innovation, and cost-effective business solutions
- To empower team members to meet customer expectations and commitments

From an organization's or department's goals flow specific business objectives and strategies for meeting them, and this is the third step in strategic planning. For example, because the IS department described above has internal customers, one of its objectives connected to exceeding customer expectations might be to lower the number of formal complaints about the system software and network and Internet connections by 80%. The strategy for accomplishing this might be (a) offering help desk support by telephone and e-mail and (b) offering training workshops and self-help materials to employee users.

The fourth step is to determine what, if any, technology might be required to advance the business strategy, and roughly estimate the resources available for technology investment. There are many facets of the technology selection decision, such as whether to develop the technology in-house or purchase it from an external vendor. Another facet is the establishment of procedures for end-user input on technology design features and specifications. Still another is doing a rough calculation of available capital for technology purchase or development. Technology selection and costing procedures are further elaborated upon in Chapter 4.

The fifth step in strategic technology planning is to measure the organization's readiness for modernization. This latter activity may be done through a survey tool, structured interviews, or a combination of the two, such as the author's Modernization Assessment for Readiness and Tracking (ModART) process. It consists of three parts. The first part is a 25-minute employee survey to obtain their perceptions of technology performance, job structure, safety, stress and satisfaction, level of involvement and influence (individual and union) in workplace change and plant operations decisions, labor relations climate, and attitudes toward workplace modernization. The second is a questionnaire given to the plant manager to collect specific plant performance measures. The third is individual interviews with members of an actual or likely joint steering committee that will guide the process of change.

A change readiness assessment is helpful for at least two reasons. One is that it helps to uncover possible problems that may thwart the success of the change effort. Attitudes toward new technology may well be reflected in employee beliefs about the degree of job control they have. The second reason is that advance assessment provides a baseline measure against which future success (or failure) can be determined.

The final, sixth step in the strategic planning process is for the strategic planning committee to put forward an action plan for achieving the goals, objectives, and strategies. This action plan should have a precise time frame and specific, achievable milestones at incremental steps of the progression. Tools such as Gantt charts and PERT flowcharts are often used for this step of strategic planning. Gantt charting is a bar graph matrix in which time (usually in months) is listed on the horizontal axis and planned activities on the vertical axis. A PERT (Program Evaluation and Review Technique) flowchart depicts the key activities needed for project completion, presented in sequential order, the estimated time for each activity, the relationships among activities, and the expected outcomes (Robbins, 1991).

Strategic planning for technology acquisition helps to ensure that the technology will in fact advance the organization's mission and business objectives and not be based merely on a vendor's recommendation or an executive officer's infatuation. Planning does not guarantee successful outcomes, but outcome success rarely occurs without planning. Still, strategic technology planning is only *part* of the framework proffered in this volume. The other piece is *partnership*. The most carefully crafted strategic plan is doomed to fail if it devised by a handful of high-level managers who develop it in isolation from the rest of the organization. All internal stakeholders described in Chapter 1 must be involved—especially frontline employees, their union representatives, and human resource managers of the company, agency, or institution.

Participation and Partnership

The concept of partnership goes beyond simply having a seat at the decision-making table. It is rooted in participation theory, which endorses direct or indirect (through elected or appointed representatives) worker involvement in decisions pertaining to the operation and governance of the organization. The levels of participation include autonomous work teams at the "bottom" of the organization, works councils, or joint labor-management committees at the department and enterprise levels, and employee or union directors on corporate boards (Jain, 1980, p. 5). Participative management goes beyond labor-management cooperation by changing power relationships. Jain (1980) explains that in contrast to the traditional hierarchical organizational model, "The participatory organizational model accepts the existence of a variety of interest groups within an enterprise, all of whom are stakeholders in it and have different goals, interests, and values . . . [and] make decisions on the basis of self interest." (p. 14)

Early Advocates of Participative Management

Employee participation in decision making is not a new idea. Although the United States lagged behind Germany, Norway, and Yugoslavia in recognizing the institutional value of joint governance, organizational theorists such as Rensis Likert and Daniel Katz saw participation as a cornerstone of the Human Relations Program they established at the University of Michigan in 1947 (Kahn, 2000). They and other researchers influenced by Kurt Lewin's theory that linked small group participation and commitment concluded that employee participation was directly related to outcomes such as productivity, adaptation to new methods of work, and lower absence and turnover (Kahn, 2000).

Earlier human relations theorists such as Harvard's Elton Mayo had set the framework for this conceptual leap with research dating back to the famous 1920s experiments at the Hawthorne Works of the giant Western Electric Company. The Hawthorne researchers had concluded that increases in worker output were connected not to physical conditions of work or to work breaks, but rather to conditions of group cohesion and status created by the experiment itself. Blumberg (1968) puts forth a third important success factor not typically cited in the literature about these experiments—the direct involvement of workers in the determination of their work tasks—a level of participation that was unheard of in the context of traditional patterns of hierarchy, power, and authority.

Cooperation Versus Partnership

Simple cooperation across labor-management or hierarchical lines does not constitute partnership. Blumberg (1968) draws a distinction between *cooperation*, in which workers receive information and can make nonbinding suggestions and *co-determination*, which has structures and processes allowing joint decision making (p. 71). Too many examples exist in the United States in which employees and their union representatives are told in advance of technological change, not for the purpose of seriously soliciting their input before key decisions are made, but rather for the purpose of appeasement and forestalling an adverse reaction.

Strategic Partnership Defined

The following, then, is the definition of strategic partnership:

A strategic partnership for the management of technological change is a goal-focused collaboration involving two or more parties operating with equal influence and mutual respect, in which they jointly plan each step of the innovation process.

The elements of a genuine labor-management partnership in a unionized workplace, applicable to technological change, can be outlined as follows:

- Early and equal participation of workplace-level union leadership in activity planning and definition
- Feasible goals, representing the respective interests of labor and management
- Mutual agreement to engage in a joint change process, and ongoing commitment to the process
- Structures for joint governance at the strategic plant or organization level
- Structures or processes for early and continuous frontline employee input (Haddad, 1997, pp. 40–41, 80–85)

Figure 2.3 offers a graphic depiction of this definition. A joint steering committee with equal representation of management and labor guides the process at the strategic level. On the management side, this is generally composed of the top-ranking on-site manager (e.g., plant manager, school principal, police chief, etc.); the human resource manager; and the managers of quality, engineering, and manufacturing or other key business units. Representing the employees in a unionized organization would typically be the bargaining council or the elected officers and union stewards. In a nonunion environment, a planning council consisting of workforce-elected representatives who volunteer to serve may play this role (Witte, 1980).

The joint steering committee devises the business strategy and technology strategy using the participative processes described earlier in this chapter (e.g., SCOT analysis and other strategic planning tools) and ensures integration of the two strategies. Because of the joint planning, committee members set forth mutually determined goals that are attainable and to which frontline employees have input through their own representative structures that interface with the steering committee. Critical to the success of the entire process is ongoing commitment to *collaboration* and *innovation*.

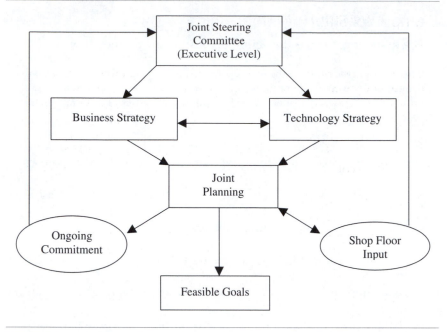

Figure 2.3   Strategic Partnership Model

Other models of strategic partnership exist. For example, a strategic partnership might occur between employers and training providers, between original equipment manufacturers (OEMs) and suppliers, and between and among various other entities involved in technology development, adoption, and use. The unique contribution of this book, though, is its focus on labor (worker and union)-management partnerships, or employee-management partnerships in nonunion settings.

As has been discussed previously in this volume, early involvement of frontline employees and their union representatives in technology decisions can yield better technology performance results. Employees with years of experience at their jobs are in a strong position to offer advice to engineers on the likely operational impact of changes in equipment design or work processes. As Brodner (1996) notes, the "complexity of products, processes and market relations" makes it imperative that management use the "knowledge, skills and expertise" of employees who are product and production experts (p. 35). The following examples further illustrate the benefits to be derived from the strategic partnership model. Each of these examples focuses on broader labor market and industry sector strategy than on technology per se.

Examples of Strategic Partnerships

CSTEC

The Canadian Steel Trade and Employment Congress (CSTEC) is a national labor-management council that was incorporated in 1986. Its purpose is to strategically address problems of trade, labor adjustment, and human resource development across the Canadian steel industry. Following some turbulent strikes in the early 1980s, national labor and management leaders recognized that it was in their respective best interests to work collaboratively on issues that went beyond the scope of collective bargaining agreements. One such issue was trade. In 1984, the U.S. government imposed quotas on the importation of Canadian steel. Canadian steel producers found that their industry association, the American Iron and Steel Institute (AISI), had little incentive to help Canadian producers in a trade war with U.S. steelmakers. Thanks to the leadership of the Canadian director of the U.S.-based union that represented their employees, the United Steelworkers of America (USWA), helped to lobby members of the U.S. Congress for a steel trade agreement.

A second strategic issue requiring bipartite collaboration was labor adjustment. Overcapacity in the Canadian steel industry had led to layoffs in the 1980s, and labor recognized it needed the cooperation of employers in finding new work for dislocated employees. Related to the dialogue about employment were discussions about technological change in the industry and job skills training for the still employed. Employment and Immigration Canada's Industrial Adjustment Service funded labor adjustment studies and assisted with employment of laid-off steelworkers (Fletcher, 1998).

The federal and provincial governments played a vital role in supporting CSTEC and other sectoral councils at the point of inception and thereafter, providing financial and staff resources for studies and direct adjustment and training services (Bradford, 1998; Haddad, 1996b). Although labor and management had themselves agreed that CSTEC should be a co-governance organization in structure and operation, government training agreements encouraged bipartite representation (Haddad, 1998) A new, more conservative Ontario government elected in 1995 abolished supportive entities such as the Ontario Training and Adjustment Board (Hayes, 1998). An 18-member joint committee oversees CSTEC's training and adjustment activities, and joint plant-level committees coordinate adjustment services and manage training programs for employed hourly and salaried workers.

Some impressive measurable outcomes illustrate CSTEC's success. From 1988 to 1994, 67 joint adjustment committees helped more than

11,000 dislocated workers, with 75% of them finding work mainly in other sectors at comparable salaries on average (Haddad, 1998). For employed workers, the joint training committees (JTCs) negotiated transfer agreements with community colleges offering courses to ensure the portability of credits earned at multiple educational institutions. More than 24,000 steelworkers received CSTEC-sponsored training in 1994–1995—after only two years of the training program's existence (Verma, Lamertz, & Warrian, 1998).

The strategic value of joint sectoral training councils goes beyond service provision to employees and dislocated workers. As Chaykowski (1998) has observed, joint sectoral councils have "pursued a distinct strategic path" through the tripartite involvement of labor, management, and government in broad, long-term human resource initiatives that extend beyond the narrow scope of workplace and collective bargaining (p. 310). The very definition of a sector council offered by the federal agency Human Resources Development Canada implies a strategic role: "a joint employer-employee organization that provides a neutral decision-making forum to determine human resource issues within the sector and to develop and implement a sectoral human resource strategy" (Gunderson & Sharpe, 1998, pp. 8–9). Chaykowski (1998) speculates, with good reason, that the information sharing and pooling of resources and the joint structures developed for training and adjustment activities could well extend into the business strategy arena (p. 310).

WRTP

Two models of strategic partnership in the human resource and business strategy domain can be found in the United States. Both are sponsored in part by the National Institute of Standards' Manufacturing Extension Partnership (NIST-MEP), a federal program designed to provide direct services to improve the competitiveness of manufacturing firms. One model is the Wisconsin Regional Training Partnership (WRTP) which combines regional labor market services with sector-specific skills training (Parker & Rogers, 1996). The Wisconsin program is an outgrowth of earlier collaboration among the state AFL-CIO, state policymakers, the vocational-technical community, and private-sector employers to establish reemployment centers for dislocated metalworkers and workplace education centers for those still employed (Governor's Commission for a Quality Workforce, 1991; Human Resources Development Institute, 1996).

The WRTP was established in 1992 with the leadership of the state labor federation president and the president of a motor castings company, and with research support from the Center on Wisconsin Strategy (COWS) at the University of Wisconsin—Madison (Human Resources

Development Institute, 1996). The jointly determined guiding principles ensured strong and equal labor involvement in the determination of skills assessment practices and skills standards, and governance of workplace education centers.

With a membership in 1998 of more than 46 firms and a host of local union affiliates of six major international unions primarily in the machining, electronics, and plastics sectors (Berth, 1997, 1998), the WRTP extended its role beyond human resource and labor market development to work directly with small and medium-size firms on modernization assessment and implementation (some nonunion firms are part of the WRTP as well). The governing board of the Wisconsin Modernization Institute, WRTP's nonprofit sponsor, has equal representation from labor and management (four representatives each), with public sector representatives (e.g., state government and technical colleges) serving as nonvoting executive council members.

Of WRTP member workplaces, 86% have joint labor-management committees that "guide the reorganization of work" (Martens & Neuenfeldt, 1997, p. 2). The WRTP employs a participatory approach that is designed to help firms and their workers help themselves following assessments and identification of internal and external resources (Berth, 1997). Two labor-management specialists from the WRTP work directly with companies and unions on a variety of labor-management and human resource issues. WRTP staff have also provided technical assistance to employers and unions on modernization projects focused on lead-time reduction, process mapping, teamwork, and training (Martens & Neuenfeldt, 1997). The WRTP has been successful in promoting a sectoral strategy that focuses on supplier network partnerships and encourages work with unionized firms (Parker & Rogers, 1996).

GIDC

Another example of a strategic partnership model is the Garment Industry Development Corporation (GIDC), a sectoral labor-management initiative that operates within a specific region. Established in 1984 as a tripartite government-labor-industry partnership, its purpose is to strengthen New York City's apparel industry by providing assistance with marketing and exporting, skills training, quality management, and engineering expertise related to the adoption of new technology and work processes (Garment Industry Development Corporation, 1995). It also maintains a domestic sourcing database to provide manufacturers with supplier and contractor capabilities (www.gidc.org). That database service and GIDC's expertise in product marketing and exporting are indicative of a strategic, forward-thinking orientation, in which labor is actively involved in business strategy. This is somewhat of an anomaly in labor-management cooperative ventures.

Employer-specific, bilingual training is provided to upgrade and diversify employee skills and career advancement prospects (Garment Industry Development Corporation, 1998). Training is available to employed and unemployed workers and management representatives. Courses for employees in such areas as computer-aided manufacturing and design, machine maintenance and repair, health and safety, supervisory skills, and workplace literacy are held at GIDC's Fashion Industry Modernization Center (FIMC), which also offers seminars and services to managers on technology and business topics (www.gidc.org). The FIMC is funded by a mix of public and private sector organizations including the State of New York, the U.S. Department of Labor, NIST, UNITE, and the Council for the American Fashion Industry Development Fund. For unemployed apparel workers, GIDC provides a job referral service, which helps to link firms with experienced employees.

GIDC is governed by a 12- to 15-member board plus chair, with equal representation from labor (UNITE—the union that resulted from the mergers of the Amalgamated Clothing and Textile Workers Union and the International Ladies Garment Workers Union), management (usually the heads of industry trade associations), and the public sector (primarily city government representatives, plus the president of the Fashion Institute of Technology (Garment Industry Development Corporation, 1998). Well over half of its 1998 budget of $2 million came from the public sector: renewed contracts with the city of New York and with the City Job Training Partnership Assistance (JTPA) program, and increasingly, funding from the state (B. Herman, personal communication, August 27, 1998). Other revenue sources include (a) a labor-management industry development fund in which participating firms contribute one tenth of payroll, (b) GIDC membership fees paid by firms, (c) contract work (for GIDC services, charged at a sliding-scale hourly rate), (d) grants from the U.S. Department of Labor and from the U.S. Department of Commerce's trade development arm (the latter for expansion of GIDC's export program), and (e) a small but growing amount of funding from private foundations (Herman, 1998).

Labor's Interest in Technology Partnerships

Both the WRTP and GIDC are union-driven, strategic models of technical assistance that place job growth and skills upgrading as core objectives of competitiveness improvement efforts. Along with CSTEC, they demonstrate that union interests extend far beyond job protectionism to engage employers and government agencies in dialogue about industrial modernization and industry growth strategies. This conclusion is supported by data collected by the author in the course of evaluating a project designed to promote collaborative technology planning at small and medium-size manufacturing firms.

In response to a written survey, 172 union leaders representing employees at small and medium-size manufacturing plants agreed that the highest priority of workplace modernization plans or activities should be high-skilled job retention or creation *and* improved plant competitiveness. This counters the popularly held view that union leaders view technological innovation through a narrow lens of self-interest.

In the same survey, they were also asked how often they are able to take a proactive role in modernization activities at plants they represent. Only 17% reported that they are "very often" or "always" able to take a proactive role, 39% replied "sometimes," and 43% stated "almost never" to "never." When asked additionally what would help them participate more proactively in workplace modernization decisions, the most frequently occurring response among the list provided was improved information sharing and communication between management, union, and shop floor employees and establishment of joint modernization committees.

A poor labor-management relationship serves as a great barrier to effective plant modernization. Case studies at 16 small and medium-size manufacturing firms engaged in modernization activity revealed that labor-management distrust can slow and even halt the progress of technological and organizational change, as can poor business management (Haddad, 2000b). Conversely, the same study found that bipartite design and implementation of workplace innovations can lead to solid, even dramatic improvements in firm performance that can be long-lasting for companies with sound business strategy and good competitive standing in the marketplace. A strategic partnership approach to technological change makes good business sense.

Summary

Organizations must strategically plan for technological change to ensure smooth implementation and to attain optimal performance results. Business and technology strategy should be integrated, and business strategy should drive technological goals. The case study from the automotive industry illustrated how technological and organizational factors worked in tandem to support strategic business objectives. Strategic business planning can be attained by use of this chapter's six-step process. A hypothetical example from higher education illustrates the first step of using an internal and external environmental scan, and a sample mission statement from a health care insurance company illustrates the second step of articulating strategic goals.

Partnership is as important as strategy to successful technology planning and implementation. The concept of partnership is rooted in participation theory and differs from simple cooperation because it requires more balanced power relationships and offers employees and their union representatives more substantive and binding decision-making authority. A strategic partnership for the management of technological change presumes early, goal-focused collaboration between parties with equal influence in which they jointly plan each step of the innovation process. This chapter presents a strategic partnership model, with an explanation of committee structure and activities. Three examples of strategic partnership involving management and unions are introduced—the CSTEC, the WRTP, and the GIDC. Both the WRTP and the GIDC were initiated by unions on a regional or sectoral basis. All three examples demonstrate that organized labor has a vested interest in industrial modernization and industry growth.

Three

An Integrative Framework for Technological Change

W hen technology introduction is planned, it progresses along a continuum of distinctive stages. The totality of this process can be thought of as a technology adoption life cycle. As used most commonly in the engineering and business literature, the term "life cycle" refers to evolutionary stages of product development. In their simplest form, these stages are "introductory," "growth," and "maturity" (Moore & Tushman, 1982, as cited in Banbury, 1999). These broad categories obscure the many steps and people it takes to move a new product from conception to design to engineering to prototype to production and finally to market or customer.

Other life cycle models refer to technology project progression (Cardullo, 1999). Ford and Ryan (1981) describe the steps and decision points a company faces when dealing with new technology as (a) development, (b) application, (c) application launch, (d) application growth, (e) technology maturity, and (f) degraded technology. It has been argued that "acquisition" is the first stage in the life cycle of any technology (Cardullo, 1999, p. 3-46). However, there are several steps that ought to precede acquisition or development, such as strategy determination, needs assessment, design, and planning.

Some would argue that business realities produce ambiguities and challenges that defy rational predictability, and that linear models are inappropriate to the hard realities of the "real world." However, there is value in outlining the logical steps to follow in order to manage the techno-logical change process, keeping in mind that progression through the stages may take place in an iterative rather than sequential manner. This is true of Goodman and Lawless' (1994) "adaptive rationality" model (p. 218), and in the life cycle model presented below.

Technology Adoption Life Cycle

Figure 3.1 presents a prescriptive model for the adoption of technological change. The first step in the technology adoption process is to identify business strategy and goals according to the strategic planning methods presented in Chapter 2. At this early point in the process, the joint steering committee reviews all of the data from the SCOT/SWOT (strengths, challenges, opportunities, threats/strengths, weaknesses, opportunities, threats) analysis and the formulation of mission and value statements, goals, objectives, and strategies. The strategic directions set forth through the planning process serve as the compass guiding all future decisions. Technology goals also become the basis against which technology success is determined during the evaluation stage.

The second step is a multidimensional assessment of whether new technology is needed to help the organization meet its business goals and objectives, and whether the organization is ready for the technology. This assessment begins with a study of existing technological and organ-izational procedures using the process called "variance analysis" (explained fully in Chapter 4) or a similar methodology. Technology selection, cost-benefit analysis, and organizational readiness are part of the needs assess-ment process.

The third step in the technology adoption life cycle is planning. At this stage the steering committee, having determined that new technology is needed and having decided whether to "build or buy" the technology, invites employees from the affected groups to participate in the develop-ment of design specifications and an implementation plan. Decisions made as a result of this process should be communicated to the workforce as a whole. A plan for training employees is also developed at this stage (more detail about how to plan and execute employee training is given in Chapter 7).

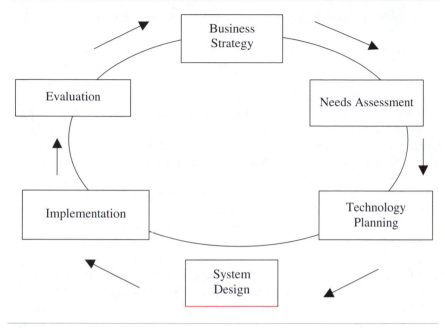

Figure 3.1   Technology Adoption Life Cycle

The next step in technology adoption is system design, where technology specifications are determined, and the vendor (if the technology is being purchased instead of built internally) is selected. One of the most frequent problems during this step is failure of the purchasing organization to negotiate with the vendor for such items as assistance with software debugging, ongoing maintenance, and training of those who will use the technology. Initial employee training may be offered at this stage (conceptual classroom training that can take place without the equipment), and the physical infrastructure is readied for the new technology's arrival (e.g., wiring, expansion of floor space through rearrangement, or surplusing of existing equipment, etc.).

The implementation stage is the actual rollout of the technology. This rollout may occur in one or more pilot departments, which is most common, or across the entire organization all at once. The obvious advantage to pilot rollout is that debugging can occur before full-scale implementation. Cross-functional implementation teams consisting of workers from the affected departments help to make decisions about the best ways to install and optimize the performance of the technology without adversely affecting employees. Hands-on training should be offered during pilot testing, before the new equipment or software is expected to be used fully.

Although evaluation is listed as the final phase of the technology adoption life cycle, it is an ongoing process. As stated earlier, technology success is determined by measuring performance against the goals and objectives that the technology is expected to meet. When the objectives are quantifiable, it is easy to determine whether the technology has fulfilled its intended purpose. Although not every objective may be quantifiable, having some that are helps to demonstrate to high-ranking managers and external constituencies that the technology has been a worthwhile investment.

For example, if a local police department has a goal of being more responsive to community needs and an objective of improving police response time by 50%, the agency may invest in automatic vehicle locator (AVL) technology. AVL is a communications system that enables a dispatcher to see precisely where police cruisers happen to be at any time so that the police vehicle that is closest to an incident can be the one sent to respond to a call. Actual response time can be measured, and any reduction can be attributed to the AVL system. However, measurable outcomes may not be the result of the technology *per se*, which makes evaluation a more difficult task than at first appearance. Police response times may have much more to do with the number of cruisers in the field during a given shift, the training of the officers, the type of incident being reported (some may require officers who are specially trained), and degree of traffic congestion on the roads.

Although evaluation of performance results is not a simple matter, it is a necessary step in the technology adoption life cycle. An organization must know whether technology has improved overall or a specific performance (e.g., quality, efficiency, safety, customer responsiveness, etc.), and whether technology has brought about tangible and intangible benefits that help to justify the cost, thereby "adding value" in ways that go beyond the accounting ledger. The information derived from the evaluation is fed back into business strategy, making the adoption life cycle a circular process.

An Integrative Systems Approach to Technology Adoption

Knowing the steps involved in the technology adoption process is important, but following them is not enough to ensure successful change. If technology is the driving force in the change process, system integration may be difficult to achieve. A review of systems theory is helpful in illustrating what is meant by system integration.

Systems Theory: An Overview

Systems theory is derived in part from biological science, with its emphasis on "hierarchically nested systems" in which components are broken down into elemental units, which, in turn, are subdivided and so on (Schilling, 2000). For example, a biological organism is "composed of organs, which are composed of cells, which contain organelles, which are composed of molecules, and so on" (Simon, 1995, p. 26, as cited in Schilling, 2000). Other disciplines have contributed to and embraced systems theory, including philosophy (Aristotle's lesson that "the whole is greater than the sum of its parts"), social science, mathematics, and technology (Jurich & Myers-Bowman, 1998), and education (Potts & Hagan, 2000).

Complex systems theory plays an important role in organizational sociology, industrial psychology, and management theory. In short, systems theory views an organization as a "living organism" with interrelated and interdependent components. Moreover, organizations are thought of as "adaptive" and "evolving" (Morel & Ramanujam, 1999) and self-regulating, even in the face of environmental instability (Vancouver, 1996). Organizations are also thought to be open systems, capable of modular recombination or "synergistic specificity" (Schilling, 2000) in which components work interactively on the specific problem at hand, as did the vehicle-specific design teams in the Amcar example presented in Chapter 1.

Sociotechnical Systems Theory

The sociotechnical systems theory of work organization illustrates the benefits of a synergistic approach to change. This theory analyzes the *technical* system used to produce goods or services, the *social* system of work organization, and the interactive effects of the two (Howarth, 1984, p. 39). Figure 3.2 offers a graphic representation of this concept. The technical system consists of physical tools, machines, and integrated systems as well as work methods and processes. The social system consists of vertical and horizontal work-related interactions, relationships, and role expectations (Taylor & Asadorian, 1985). This system also refers to the way in which work is organized, the structure of jobs and of the organization, organizational culture, human resource management practices, and labor relations. The areas of intersection are representative of *systems integration* or *joint optimization*—the symbiotic relationship that is meant to occur as the two interdependent systems interact.

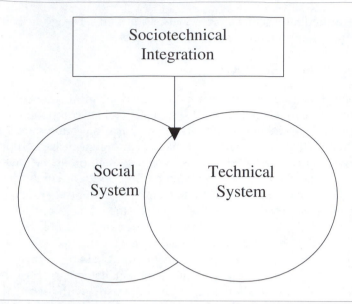

Figure 3.2   Sociotechnical Systems Integration

Sociotechnical systems theory owes its origin to field research conducted in 1949 in the newly nationalized coal mines of postwar Great Britain. Eric Trist, a psychologist with London's Tavistock Institute of Human Relations, and Kenneth Bamforth, a postgraduate fellow who had spent 18 years as a coal miner before entering academe, set out to discover why productivity and morale lagged with increased automation (Trist, 1981).

The "hand-got" method of extracting coal in "shortwall" rock faces in use before mechanization consisted of autonomous work groups of two skilled men, assisted by one or more laborers. The miners were multi-skilled and able to exchange tasks with one another, and they operated with minimal external supervision. Trist (1981) characterized the atmosphere as being cooperative, with high personal commitment and productivity and low absenteeism and infrequent accidents.

This contrasted dramatically with the "longwall" method of extraction made possible by mechanization, which involved mining a single long rock face instead of a series of short faces. The mechanization required the work to be reorganized into much larger units of about fifty men, with each worker performing a different set of job tasks. Coordination and control became the province of supervisors who were external to the work groups, and who exerted some degree of coercion (Trist, 1981). Trist and Bamforth (1951) found that the mass production nature of the longwall method created high-productivity expectations, increased competitiveness and individualism within and between work units, broke down group cohesiveness, and increased absenteeism. The lesson learned from this study was that it is unwise to make changes in the technical system of an organization without paying sufficient attention to its likely effect on the preexisting social system.

Sociotechnical systems (STS) integration is both a *theory* and a *method* of work design or redesign. Unlike job enrichment schemes, sociotechnical systems redesign focuses on the work system, not on the individual job (Trist, 1981, p. 21). Its three basic principles are as follows:

1. Joint optimization—seeking the best fit between the technical and social systems.

2. Open systems planning—establishing feedback mechanisms to allow the social and technical systems to improve and adapt to changing environmental requirements.

3. Participation—allowing employees to participate in the analysis and design the structure of their work (Bancroft, 1992, pp. 41–43).

This latter aspect is stated more strongly by Taylor and Felten (1993) who discuss the need for an "empowered" workforce that is in control of the product or service and the methods for generating it (p. 7). Taylor and Felten argue that although managers must be empowered to deal with strategy and long-term tasks, the workforce also must be involved in long-term decisions and strategy formulation.

The basic steps involved in STS work design are outlined in Table 3.1.

Sociotechnical systems work redesign was popular in Scandinavia, particularly in Sweden and Norway, as early as the 1960s. The Volvo Uddevalla automobile factory in Sweden was for many years a model of sociotechnical manufacturing success. Other notable examples were Shell petrochemical plants in Great Britain and Canada and a Cummins Engine plant in the United States (Trist, 1981). The U.S. importation of STS coincided with the "Quality of Work Life" movement, which was thought to be an antidote to worker alienation evident in large manufacturing plants with routinized, low-skill operations.

Advocates of "lean production" have pointed to the closure of the Udevalla plant as proof that sociotechnical systems design cannot compete in today's highly competitive market. "Lean production" refers to the Japanese manufacturing system heralded by Womack, Jones, and Roos (1990) that relies on short production cycle time, reduced inventory, and work teams, among other organizational factors to attain high levels of efficiency and quality. Yet a professor of operations management at

Table 3.1   STS Work Design Steps

Step	Process
1.	Scanning: mapping out an overview of the system that transforms inputs to outputs within a bounded area (a specific workplace or department), including personnel.
2.	Identification of unit operations: those processes that transform a material, product, or service within the target area.
3.	Discovery of key variances (deviations from the norm that significantly affect the quality or quantity of the operation) and their interrelations.
4.	Drawing up a table of variance control to determine how much the key variances are controlled by the social system (workers, supervisors, and managers) and whether any are imported or exported across units or departments.
5.	Mapping out linear role relationships (vertical and horizontal) in the target unit.
6.	Analysis of employees' (workers, managers, supervisors) perceptions of their roles and their possibilities, plus constraining factors.
7.	Analysis of the role relationships of employees with those of neighboring systems (e.g., support and maintenance) and boundary-crossing systems (supplier & user systems).
8.	Examination of the general management system and the effects of technical or social policies or plans.
9.	Design proposals for the target and/or neighboring systems.

SOURCE: Trist (1981) and Taylor (1975).

Sweden's Chalmers University of Technology argues that certain aspects of the Japanese and Swedish systems (e.g., total quality management, total productive maintenance, teamwork, and participation) are compatible especially in product development engineering, adding that the Udevalla closing was because of a sales decline and the increased role of suppliers in subassembly (Karlsson, 1995). Berggren (1992) echoes this view, pointing to the fact that the supplier industry for the Volvo, which accounts for "75% of the value of a car," lacked the quality and commitment of the Japanese components sector (p. 165).

Indeed, the concurrent engineering philosophy that guided Amcar's strategy of shortening product development time represented sociotechnical systems integration, because organizational and technological changes in the engineering operation occurred in tandem and complimented one another. Citing the work of another researcher, Karlsson (1995) notes that in product engineering operations "most technical problems are solved in the social system" (p. 55). Haddad's (1996a) findings affirm this view, but her research also points to the value of communications technologies that supported the work of product development teams.

Some organizations find it difficult to implement sociotechnical systems integration for any or all of the following reasons:

BARRIERS TO STS INTEGRATION

- Narrow orientation of people from different functional groups
- Technological determinism practiced
- Organizational culture not conducive to participation
- Lack of empowerment of employees
- Lack of business manager familiarity with technology

Sociotechnical systems theory is the antithesis of scientific management— not only because it allows employee participation in work redesign, but also because under joint optimization the technical system cannot lead the change effort in a deterministic way, thereby forcing the social system to adapt to it (Trist, 1981). Rather, new technology is meant to be "human centered" rather than technology driven (Badham, 1995, p. 86). Howarth (1984), too, emphasizes this latter point as she outlines some principles that have guided more recent sociotechnical work design/redesign efforts:

1. If an organization follows the dictates of the technical system at the expense of the social (or vice versa), the good results hoped for will not be achieved.

2. For any one technical system a whole range of workable social systems is possible.

3. The use of cohesive, autonomous groups as the base of the social system offers great advantages in terms of the satisfaction and commitment of the workers, and, therefore, in terms of productivity.

4. For best results, it is preferable to design (or redesign) the technical and social systems together (originally the technical system is taken as given and the social system redesigned to give improved results, but more recently it has become clear that better results can be achieved if the technical system is improved, or chosen, in conjunction with the social system).

5. An organization (or "sociotechnical system") cannot be isolated from the environment in which it operates (the so-called open systems approach); sociotechnical analysis therefore now incorporates the relationship between an organization and its environment, taking into account how changes in the world of work affect society and how changes in society affect the world of work.

6. Relevant trade unions should be fully involved in research and experimental projects and where possible the workers affected by changes should also have a say in their formulation (again this was not originally typical of the sociotechnical approach, but recently its importance has become more apparent—possibly because a good deal of the more recent work has been done in Norway and Sweden with their national emphasis on industrial democracy and participation). (pp. 41–42)

Industrial Relations Theory

As Howarth (1984) indicates, and as mentioned in Chapter 2, the labor-management relationship is key to successful technology adoption in a framework of sociotechnical integration. An industrial relations perspective goes beyond management theories designed to humanize work and "leads us to consider human resource practices from the point of view of all the stakeholders to an employment relationship" (Kochan, 1996, p. 250). Greater complexity in labor-management structures and processes has changed the nature of collective bargaining; whereas in the past there were regular, formal bilateral negotiations, now in many cases there are "multilateral arrangements as customers, stockholders, communities and others seek to influence labor-management negotiations" (Walton, Cutcher-Gershenfeld, & McKersie, 1994, p. viii).

To not regard labor unions and the employees they represent as one of many stakeholders in work redesign is to miss an opportunity for strategic, joint collaboration that is a prerequisite to fundamental and lasting change. Unions serve as a "collective voice" and create conditions for ongoing input and improvement of management practices (Cooke, 1994). Although proponents of sociotechnical systems in the United States have "largely ignored" the role of unions both in theory and practice, "true union engagement is a necessity" for STS "to have the breadth of impact it should" (Cohen-Rosenthal, 1997, pp. 585, 602). This collaboration requires employee and union input upfront at the problem analysis and solution design stages. Thus, the strategic dimension of partnership advocated in this volume falls between sociotechnical systems theory, which is focused primarily on the internal organization, and strategic management theory, in which external factors play a role in the formulation of business strategy

(Dunphy, 1996). It is vital that organizational structures for joint decision making be included in collective bargaining agreements with unions and embedded in the day-to-day operation of the organization, so that joint decision making does not become merely a passing fad or "flavor of the month"—to use the parlance of union leaders who have seen employee involvement programs come and go. Participative change that is systemic rather than piecemeal can result in improved business productivity and performance (Ichiniowski et al., 1996).

The formal labor-management relationship converges around the regular negotiation of the terms and conditions of employment, which are codified in a collective bargaining agreement, and the subsequent administration and enforcement of that agreement. Yet in the United States, decisions about capital investment and efficiency improvements are legally within the scope of management rights, and bilateral agreement in advance of the change is not required (Finzel & Abraham, 1996). For this reason, when unions are successful in negotiating technological change provisions, the language is far more likely to be "protectionist" (e.g., concerning advance notification, seniority governing layoff, income protection), than "future oriented" (Solomon, 1987, p. 53).

In contrast, a strategic partnership approach to technological change in a unionized workplace is based on negotiated provisions that create joint structures at the top and bottom levels of the organization. These strategic and departmental joint committees serve as forums for union and worker "involvement" in "decisions about technology choice, appropriate technologies, selection of hardware and software, selection and role of vendors, workplace redesign, software programming and training" (Haddad, 1989, pp. 60–61). Proactive union involvement in technological change is consistent with a technology management paradigm premised on open systems theory (Liker, Haddad, & Karlin, 1999), in which the organization is ever evolving through its interactions with the external environment. To be effective in this role, workplace-level union leaders may need technical assistance or training in technology needs assessment, planning, design (including ergonomic fit), and evaluation.

Case Study: Professional Paper Company—Westward Mill

A paper mill (referred to here by the pseudonym "Westward Mill"), in operation since 1903 and employing more than 300 employees, produces specialty text and cover papers for greeting cards, textbooks, blueprints, and archival papers, as well as watermarked writing papers for domestic and international markets. In one recent year, 7,000 tons of paper were produced. Mill operations include pulp preparation (addition of water, dyes, fillers, and other materials to make the needed paper), conversion (feeding the prepared pulp mixture into large paper machines for pressing, rolling, drying, and coating), finishing (sheeting, embossing, sorting, inspection, and packing), and shipping.

The mill is unionized, and the most recent collective bargaining agreement contained language establishing a strategic-level joint committee with the intent of establishing self-directed work teams. The "Memorandum of Understanding" read as follows:

> The Union and the Company agree that the development of Self Managed work teams at the Westward Mill are [sic] necessary for the Westward Mill to reach and maintain a World Class competitive position in the future. The objectives of this change in working relationships are expected to make the Mill operation more productive, produce higher quality of products, and reduce overall costs of manufacturing. The parties realize that utilizing the skills and experience of all employees working together to produce products that meet the highest quality standards and provide the highest customer service will result in the highest returns for the Company and its employees and the greatest work security for all.
>
> The parties agree to form a joint implementation/oversight team of four production employees selected by the Union and four management employees to develop a plan to move the mill toward establishment of self directed work teams that are designed to obtain the stated objectives. The committee will be designated by the parties within 30 days following ratification of this agreement.
>
> Examples of the issues that the committee will be expected to make recommendations on include:
>
> team designations
>
> team responsibilities
>
> training requirements
>
> information requirements
>
> communications options
>
> necessary other resources.
>
> Outside consultants may be used by the committee to assist them in these efforts.
>
> The Union and Company will work together to develop a mutually acceptable implementation plan and mutually agree to any alterations of the labor agreement that may be necessary. The Company will pay the members of this committee for the time while attending meetings at the appropriate rate.

The movement into work teams described here at Westward Mill was seen as a way to increase productivity to compensate for the parent company's inadequate investment in capital improvements. Although capital investment and new product development expenditures had increased for a time, there was a recent drop of 50% in such spending, and the parent company placed greater priority on reducing costs than on making additional investments.

A maintenance supervisor was convinced that self-directed work teams would indeed improve mill performance:

> I think if you give people responsibility it's a wonder how much ownership they can take on their job, and how much improvement you can make . . . To me, it's too bad we're so late in doing this. We have only scratched the tip of the iceberg on how profitable this plant can be. It's gonna be scary how much money we're gonna make in a couple years. Our owners should be very pleased.

A consultant (this author was involved not as the consultant but as a project evaluator) acceptable to both parties was hired by the company (a grant application to the state was not funded) to conduct team-building and problem-solving training for members of the joint implementation/oversight team and departmental work teams (twenty 4-hour sessions were planned for shop floor employees). Before the first departmental pilot work team was selected and trained, the consultant surveyed a sample of hourly and salaried employees and conducted structured interviews with a sample of managers, union representatives, and plant employees who were, for the most part, members of the joint implementation/oversight team.

On the positive side, this assessment revealed above-average job satisfaction and autonomy, safety and ergonomics, attitudes toward modernization, willingness to work harder to help the company succeed, and a belief in a "good future with the company." Areas in need of improvement were communication, lack of employee consultation and participation in workplace change decisions, low trust and poor labor relations in some departments, lack of training beyond the minimum, high absenteeism, supervisor job dissatisfaction, and management's lack of follow through in enforcing work standards, equitable treatment, and rewarding employees for suggestions or extra effort.

The valuable information gleaned from this assessment was used not only to help determine topics for team training but also to make immediate changes. A reward and recognition program with sizable cash rewards was instituted, and to improve communication, the mill instituted meetings every other month that were attended, in shifts, by all employees. These meetings were used to communicate important information about product development, sales, and other business matters and gave employees opportunities to ask questions about mill performance and planning. Another immediate change was an agreement between the company and union for advance consultation with the joint safety and ergonomics committee along with representatives from maintenance before purchasing new machines or tools.

As part of its training, the joint implementation/oversight team contacted and visited unionized plants that had successfully transitioned to self-directed work teams. Team members communicated their findings to plant employees at one of the regularly scheduled plant meetings. Westward Mill established two primary criteria for the selection of a pilot area for implementing the first self-directed team: (a) an already functioning interdependent team due to the nature of the work (e.g., paper machines, packaging line) and (b) amicable labor relations (as measured by grievance rate and aforementioned survey assessment).

Among the accomplishments of the mill following the movement to self-directed work teams were these:

- Successful implementation of a new sheeting machine whereby operators and maintenance employees had input in the evaluation prior to purchase, trades employees were involved in set-up and debugging, and operators were trained before full production was required.
- Involvement of 20 hourly and salaried employees on a product development team that created a new, high-quality laser paper from recycled material.
- Successful use of computerized paper measurement equipment that paper tenders initially feared, following hands-on training and learning.
- Improved production cycle time and quicker shipment of product to customers.
- Implementation of a gain-sharing incentive program.
- Meeting of certification standards (ISO 9000) regarding paper product quality and consistency.
- Increased willingness on the part of the parent company to invest more money in capital improvements.
- A more positive organizational culture as a result of these changes.

The cooperative relationship between plant managers and union representatives was a major factor in the successful transition to self-directed work teams, mill performance improvements, and ultimately in capital investment. While labor relations *per se* is not enough to guarantee business success, a poor labor-management relationship is certain to derail performance.

Case Study: Shiny Metal

A second case study that for a time came close to illustrating the benefits of labor-management partnership, albeit short term, involved a small plant (which will go by the pseudonym of "Shiny Metal") that benefited from an external strategy-based modernization intervention. The plant, a producer of metal frames for industrial displays and parts for vending machines and medical equipment, employed 38 people at the outset of the intervention, which was down from a workforce high of 200 in the mid-1980s. With dropping sales and poor economic performance, Shiny Metal sought assistance from a regional manufacturing extension center (MEC)[1] whose technical field agent consultant (an engineer by training) tried to improve production flow and delivery time, and lower costs by redesigning the plant layout. However, the local labor union mistrusted plant management and the consultant, and the latter's attempts to make changes in work processes were formally grieved. In fact, labor-management acrimony became so intense that the parties at one point communicated by intercom rather than sit in the same room with each other.

It was at this point that the MEC project manager referred the case to the coordinator of a special intervention project called "Labor Participation in Modernization" (LPIM), which was designed to promote cooperative and jointly conceived modernization improvements through early involvement of the union in the design of the change (this author served as the evaluator of that project). A field agent with expertise as a labor union practitioner and a graduate degree in business administration agreed to get involved. With the intervention of national and regional union staff representatives who supported the LPIM, the agent was able to arrange a meeting with the union's elected local leaders and plant employees to solicit their input on how to rectify the problems facing the plant.

Management was impressed with the union's subsequent improvement list and suggested some additional items of its own. The two parties, operating informally as a joint steering committee with the facilitation of the MEC labor expert, drafted a vision statement of what the company should look like four years later. After a series of meetings, the steering committee determined that self-directed work teams would help to improve process flow. The labor expert ensured that the union had access to relevant business and financial information, and that they had equal input on the design and implementation of the work team and process flow changes. Supervisors were removed from the shop floor and replaced by bargaining-unit "group leaders," and the self-directed teams assumed the tasks of production scheduling, workflow coordination, and quality monitoring.

Although a few workers resisted these changes, the local union leaders encouraged employee buy in, and improvements in throughput time and product quality were soon evident. Within a few months, sales increased by 28% over the previous year, shipments to customers increased 150% in a 3-week period, new products were introduced, lending agencies extended the plant's line of credit, and employment increased to more than 100 employees. Laid-off employees were called back to work, and new hires were added to the workforce. Employee attitudes and morale markedly improved, and the number of grievances filed against the company dropped by 90%.

Unfortunately, the turnaround of the plant was not sustained. The company president obstructed certain technical changes suggested by the engineering consultant and the union members, and created labor-management acrimony by refusing to pay employees for time not worked because of a power failure. Local union leaders asked that supervisors be returned to the plant so that group leaders would not be forced to document the performance shortcomings of fellow employees. Cash flow problems created by a major customer's failure to remit payment for products on a timely basis crippled the plant's ability to purchase needed raw materials and supplies, which in turn led to lost sales and workforce layoffs. Ultimately, the plant closed and declared bankruptcy.

These two cases are markedly different in objectives and outcomes. At Shiny Metal, the change was born of crisis, while at Westward Mill it was driven by opportunity. Yet both cases illustrate the link between labor-management partnership and integrative change. Although a positive labor relationship is not enough to ensure good business performance or to overcome poor managerial decisions, it is nonetheless a prerequisite to lasting organizational performance improvement.

Summary

This chapter presented a technology life cycle model that progresses from strategic needs assessment to planning and design to implementation and evaluation. Underlying this model is the concept of sociotechnical systems (STS) integration. STS is derived from systems theory integration and refers to a smooth interface of the technical tools, machines, methods, and processes with the human and organizational roles, relationships, and structures. STS is not only a theory but also a method of work redesign that seeks to optimize the fit between the technical and social systems through open systems planning and adjustment and through the participation of employees in work analysis and design. Sociotechnical principles have been applied to workplaces in the United States, Canada, and Europe.

The labor-management relationship is key to the successful adoption of new technology in a sociotechnical framework. The most robust structures are joint committees at the top and bottom levels of the organization, codified in the collective bargaining agreement. The "Westward Mill" is an example of a company that joined forces with its union to negotiate provisions for self-managed work teams. These teams implemented new machinery according to the partnership principles advocated in this book and also worked on the development of a new product, improved cycle and delivery times and product quality, and implemented a gain-sharing program. A more positive work culture resulted as well.

A second example, from the "Shiny Metal" plant illustrated the benefits of labor-management partnership, if only for a short time. With the support of an external intervention agency, the plant instituted an informal joint steering committee, developed a mission statement, and implemented self-directed work teams that assumed responsibility for production scheduling, workflow coordination, and quality monitoring. Dramatic improvements in product delivery and consequently in sales resulted, leading to increases in the size of the workforce. The labor-management relationship improved as well. Ultimately, unilateral actions by plant management led to business problems, soured labor relations, and resulted in plant closure. A good labor relationship is not enough to compensate for poor business decisions, but a poor relationship will generally lead to problems with technology adoption and operation—even at financially healthy workplaces.

Note

1. A Manufacturing Extension Center is an institute, funded in part by the National Institute of Technology and Standards and Technology's Manufacturing Extension Partnership (NIST-MEP) program, designed to improve the competitiveness of small and medium-size (< 500 employees) manufacturing firms by providing them with technical assistance in modernization and other performance enhancing innovations.

Four

Assessing the Need and Readiness for Change

Ew technology has a certain appeal, and sometimes investing in it is motivated by "techno-lust"—an attraction to its "bells and whistles" that precludes rational analysis of whether or not the technology will help the organization meet its performance and business objectives. Needs analysis and readiness for change analysis are two distinct facets of the needs assessment life cycle stage described in Chapter 3.

Needs analysis involves the following:

- Identifying the most pressing business and organizational goals (using methods described in Chapter 2)
- Analyzing current performance to determine how well the organization is meeting these goals
- Determining whether new technology will help in the attainment of the goals
- Identifying the precise type(s) and amount of technology needed
- Calculating the costs and benefits of the technology to be acquired
- Having in place a measurable process for assessing whether the technology is meeting its performance objectives

Readiness-for-change analysis involves the following:

- Reviewing past technology implementation practices for evidence of success or failure and the reasons for such outcomes
- Analyzing current organizational culture, labor relations, job design, and other aspects of organizational readiness for change
- Assessing the capability of the physical and technical infrastructure to accommodate the new technology
- Outlining a general plan for skill assessment and training

Technology Needs Analysis

Reasons for Acquiring New Technology

Those who have the power to make decisions about the acquisition of new technology should have unambiguous reasons for doing so. The framework appearing as Table 4.1 can serve as a checklist of possible business and organizational performance needs. The specific goals necessarily vary by industry (e.g., "defects" relates to manufactured products and "student test scores" pertains to schools).

Variance Analysis Methodology

After identifying business and organizational goals, organizations must analyze current performance to determine how well the company/agency/school is meeting its goals. A useful process for doing so is "variance analysis" (Taylor & Asadorian, 1985)—a methodology used in sociotechnical systems (STS) design, a philosophy and practice that was discussed in Chapter 3. It involves mapping out all manufacturing or service operations, breaking down each element into measurable inputs and outputs, and determining the key technical and social/organizational variances at each operational step. Key variances are those that reoccur at various stages of the process or that have a significant adverse effect on product/service quality, safety, productivity, quality of working life, or other factors central to the mission and goals of the organization. Variances are determined through physical observation and interviews with employees from operations, maintenance, technical/information services, and management.

Table 4.2 illustrates what a simplified variance analysis might resemble for a fictitious hospital treating an automobile accident victim. The number of variances has been exaggerated to illustrate the various technological and organizational causes of problems that might occur. Other liberties have been taken as well. Sociotechnical systems advocates do not

Table 4.1   Reasons for Acquiring New Technology

Underlying Broad Goal	Specific Goal
Efficiency	• Increased productivity (ratio of output to input) • Reduced setup time • Reduced throughput time • Improved delivery time
Cost	• Reduced inventory • Reduced scrap/wasted time • Value-added benefits such as broader customer base
Product/Service Quality	• Product/service consistency • Fewer defects/customer complaints • High customer satisfaction • Higher student test scores • Reputation in the marketplace
Flexibility	• Customized products/services • Ability to increase volume of output during peak periods • Ability to modify/customize product or service
Health and Safety	• Lower accident and injury rates • Lower incidence of health ailments and disease • Improved workstation comfort
Quality of Working Life	• High-skilled jobs • Improved job satisfaction • Lower absenteeism • High employee retention • Job creation
Market Share/Public Sector Accountability	• Reduced product/service development cycle • New products/services offered

regard variances as problems *per se*, but rather as "deviation[s] from normal, expected or average state of the throughput" (Taylor & Felten, 1993, p. 59). Moreover, an actual variance analysis would provide detail on precisely where the variance occurred, where and by whom it was meant to be controlled, the activities needed to control it, and suggestions for needed changes in job/organization design and in the technology (Taylor & Felten, 1993, pp. 86–87).

Table 4.2   Simplified Variance Analysis at Hospital X

	Procedure	Variance	Cause
1	Patient admitted to emergency	Two-hour wait in emergency room	• Inaccurate information in database about number of available beds • Shortage of medical intake staff
2	LPN checks temperature & blood pressure	Inaccurate blood pressure reading	• Blood pressure cuff is wrong size for patient's arm
3	Physical exam by doctor	Doctor cannot communicate fully with patient	• Patient's hearing aid has fallen into hospital bedding
4	Nurse treats superficial wounds	No pain medication administered	• Doctor gave a verbal order for medication but it was never written in chart
5	Patient sent to x-ray	Patient has to be moved multiple times to get needed x-rays	• Design of x-ray equipment requires patient mobility
6	Patient admitted to hospital	Placed in shared room with patient who has a viral infection	• Viral infection not recorded in patient database
7	Orthopedic surgery scheduled for fractured hip	Surgery date is two weeks from date of accident	• Surgeon unwilling to change surgery dates of other patients
8	Surgery performed	Nails for hip pinning are out-of-stock	• Inventory and supply shortage
9	Postoperative recovery	Two conflicting pain medications administered; dramatic drop in blood pressure	• Nurse shift rotation • Failure to record one of medications in chart
10	Rehabilitation/ physical therapy	Pain and swelling of surgery site limits effectiveness of physical therapy	• Doctor slow to prescribe adequate pain medication • Health plan limits days of physical therapy
11	Determination of home care needs	Social worker recommends home health aide	• Medical insurance does not provide this benefit
12	Patient released	Patient falls in home within two days of release	• Patient unable to care for self • Patient discharged with crutches instead of walker

A variance analysis can point to technology shortcomings or needs. In the hospital example, it would appear that a more mobile X-ray machine requiring less patient repositioning would be a useful acquisition. Still, it is clear from the information in Table 4.2 that the hospital's problems go beyond its technology. Staffing, communication, equipment mainte-nance, training, and supply inventory control are additional areas in need of fixing.

Technology Needs Analysis Questions

Once the variance analysis is completed, a host of questions are used to advance the technology needs analysis. The last question in the following list (#8) goes beyond basic needs analysis by addressing the issue of organ-izational readiness for change.

1. Will a redesign of existing operations eliminate the problem or permit the organization to pursue a market opportunity?

2. Is there a form of technology (hardware or software) available on the market that meets the organization's needs?

3. If not, can the organization work with a vendor or internal team to design one?

4. What are the overt and hidden costs of the new equipment?

5. What are the measurable and intangible benefits that might justify the cost?

6. Will the technology require additional personnel, training, compen-sation or changes in procedures/work practices?

7. Can the physical infrastructure accommodate the new technology?

8. Is the organization ready for new technology?

Conducting a cross-impact analysis is a good way to round out the technology needs analysis process. This forecasting method involves the development of a matrix to determine new technology's predicted impact on products/services, processes, and other technologies (Goodman & Lawless, 1994, pp. 212–213). Although the impact on employees in the organization is not mentioned by Goodman and Lawless, clearly this should be an added part of the matrix.

Shopping for Technology

Locating the technology that is most appropriate to the organization's goals and needs requires advance research. As with the purchase of a big-ticket consumer item, such as an automobile, it is best to follow these steps:

- Draw up a list of necessary and desired features.
- Identify through reading and shopping a subset of technologies that have those features.
- Conduct research on the subset of technology options to determine customer satisfaction and consumer ratings of reliability and performance.
- Comparison shop for the best price, terms, and service.

There are numerous ways to discover technologies that are appropriate to an organization's needs, including reading trade journals, attending trade shows, visiting vendor sites, and discussing appropriate technologies with members of professional associations in the same industry. Learning about the latest technologies has benefits that go beyond possible acquisition of them. During a research visit to a small plant manufacturing high-end commercial stoves, this author discovered that the plant-level union representatives regularly attended industry trade shows at their own expense to learn about the products of competitor firms in order to better understand their plant's position in the market place. Knowing that their stoves were of a higher quality also allowed the plant representative to take greater pride in their product.

Sometimes it is more effective to design and build the technology "in-house" or subcontract the fabrication process to a firm hired for this purpose. In either case, it is strongly advised that end-users, maintenance and technical employees, health and safety committee members, and trainers be involved in determining or reviewing design specifications and in prototype testing. When purchasing the technology, it can be beneficial for the organization to negotiate a lease or test period at its own facility, to ensure that the technology works as well there as it does at the vendor's site. Unforeseen factors like heating and cooling temperatures can affect the performance of some equipment.

A southeast Michigan community's department of public safety uses a proactive approach to researching new technology. An equipment and technology standing committee, consisting of all major classifications of employees (e.g., police officers, dispatchers, clerks, and a supervisor who acts as facilitator) meets proactively on a regular basis to identify and evaluate products and systems that relate to emerging needs of the police department. They convey to the agency information about what is available, and, if a particular item seems promising, a study group is formed from the equipment committee, plus information systems and finance department representatives.

This study group assesses the needs of prospective users, discusses with the unions concerns that they may have, determines specifications, meets with vendors, and rates the technologies studied. Their report serves as a basis for the procurement of funds for technology purchase.

Vendor-provided training (initial and follow-up) and ongoing system support are typically built into the purchase agreement. These procedures were used, for example, to replace mobile data terminals in patrol cars with laptop computers, and to adopt a new records system and in-car video cameras.

Cost-Benefit Analysis

Although well-chosen manufacturing technology should be considered an investment in the future rather than an expense (Gaynor, 1990, pp. 166–167), calculating rough costs and estimating likely benefits prior to technology purchase is a necessary and prudent exercise. Traditional accounting methods that use direct labor as a basis for allocating overhead expenses to production costs discourage technology investment and are inappropriate in today's automated environment in which labor is a smaller percentage of overall cost (Gaynor, 1990; Noori, 1990, p. 193).

An arguably more appropriate accounting alternative combines activity-based costing (ABC) with economic value-added (EVA) estimation (Roztocki & Needy, 1999). This approach involves the following steps:

1. Review the company's financial information (e.g., from the income and balance sheet, comparing assets and liabilities).

2. Identify the main business activities of the organization (e.g., marketing, engineering, purchasing, etc.) and specific activities associated with each (e.g., contacting customers, preparing quotes, invoicing, and collecting money).

3. Calculate the operating cost for each specific activity.

4. Determine the capital charge for each activity by converting balance sheet data into capital costs or charges, which are then added to the cost for each activity as calculated in Step 3.

5. Determine drivers of operating and capital costs (e.g., an operating cost driver for the activity of materials receiving and handling would be the number of receipts, and the capital cost driver might be the dollar value of received material plus the time materials wait to be processed).

6. Calculate product cost (trace operating and capital costs to the products/services) (Roztocki & Needy, 1999, p. 18)

Advocates of this method of cost estimation believe that it encourages managers to make decisions that will promote long-term economic value rather than generate short-term profit (Roztocki & Needy, 1999, p. 21).

In thinking about cost-benefit analysis, it is useful to draw a distinction between "tangible" and "intangible" costs and benefits. Tangible items

Table 4.3   Tangible and Intangible Costs and Benefits Associated with New Technology

Tangible Costs	Intangible Costs
• Purchase price of technology	• Machine/system downtime
• Installation	• Site preparation
• Operating cost (energy)	• Technology inflexibility
• Maintenance	• Cost of adjusting support functions
• Training	• Negotiated pay increases

Tangible Benefits	Intangible Benefits
• Higher productivity	• More time for customer service
• Improved product/service quality	• Improved consumer confidence
• Fewer job-related injuries	• Higher worker morale
• Higher sales/increased market share	• Greater flexibility to pursue new markets
• Increased ability to customize products/services	• Faster response time to market demand

are those that are easy to predict and quantify, while intangible costs and benefits are those that are not as predictable or measurable. Gaynor (1990) notes that the ultimate goal is to make the intangible benefits of technology investment tangible (p. 168). For example, customer satisfaction is an intangible benefit (unless surveys are conducted) that may arise out of new technology investment. However, this may well translate into increased sales/business, which is a tangible benefit. Table 4.3 presents some typical costs and benefits involved with the purchase of new technology. Noori (1990) presents a similar list (pp. 203–205).

Seven-Step Technology Cost-Benefit Justification Process

The following seven-step process is recommended as a starting point for technology cost-benefit justification. A hypothetical example concerning a university department's purchase of two new instructional videos is offered to illustrate each of the seven points.

1. Identify technology type. (Two new instructional videos on high-performance work systems are needed by the university department.)

2. Justify the concept. (The videos are needed to illustrate key concepts in technology management graduate courses; student course evaluation feedback suggests benefit of case study illustrations.)

3. Justify the technology needed. (The videos identified fit into thematic units in two different graduate courses.)

4. Identify the tangible costs. (The purchase cost of the two videos.)

5. Identify the intangible costs. (The single VCR machine in the department may be insufficient for increased use.)

6. Identify the tangible benefits. (Greater variety in teaching methods likely to result in more positive student course ratings.)

7. Identify the intangible benefits. (The videos leave a more lasting visual impression than text-based case studies; student identification with issues raised in films.)

Readiness for Change Assessment

Why Measure Change Readiness?

A readiness-for-change assessment has multifaceted value. First, it helps to determine whether or not serious internal obstacles exist that might diminish the effectiveness of the change—in this case new technology. Internal obstacles may take the form of

- attitudes (individual, group, culture);
- organizational structure (e.g., composition of departments, levels of hierarchy, job design);
- physical infrastructure (e.g., size of facility, wiring for new hardware, physical capacity to run new equipment);
- human resources (e.g., adequacy of personnel, skills, compensation);
- governance (e.g., degree of participation, labor relations);
- financial resources (e.g., resources that can be devoted to new technology and related costs); and
- technical skill (e.g., level of resident technical expertise).

Second, a readiness-for-change audit helps identify readiness variances among departments and subpopulations thereby providing valuable information to steering committee members as they decide where to pilot test the new technology. Third, it can be a source of information on self-reported or tested training needs. Finally, measuring change readiness prior to technology implementation provides a baseline against which future progress can be compared.

How to Measure Change Readiness

An organization can engage in its own self-study using action research methodology under the guidance of a trained internal organizational development/human resource professional or external consultant. A consultant who is jointly selected by labor and management can bring a level of objectivity and dispassion to the process that can be helpful—especially in a workplace with a history of labor-management distrust or poor employee morale. As with the Hawthorne experiments described in Chapter 2, interviews conducted by outsiders can have a cathartic value, and employees may feel more comfortable about revealing their views to external researchers who hold no power in the organization.

Action research is the name of a methodology in which employee representatives participate directly in the research design and in the data collection process of their own self-study (Whyte, 1991). Although members of the joint steering committee will be centrally involved, there should also be input from frontline employees.

Typically the methods for assessing change readiness are (a) interviews with a small sample of personnel representing a cross-section of the organization (including the steering committee) and (b) a survey of a larger representative sample of employees. To glean a thorough picture of organizational climate, the survey should cover areas similar to those in the author's Modernization Assessment for Readiness and Tracking (ModART) tool (mentioned in Chapter 2):

- Employee perceptions of technology performance
- Attitudes toward workplace modernization
- Job structure and degree of discretion
- Job safety
- Job stress
- Job satisfaction
- Managerial communication
- Adequacy of training
- Performance recognition
- Level of involvement and influence (individual and union) in workplace change and plant operations decisions
- Labor relations climate

As a starting point, the reader may find it useful to complete the questionnaire in Box 4.1. Although it is no substitute for a more thorough organizational assessment survey, it can help an organization's leaders anticipate possible enablers of and barriers to technological change

Pragmatic Issues

Assessing the need and readiness for technological change according to the methods described in this chapter is highly advisable, but not always feasible. There are times when the need to introduce new technology is so compelling that a lengthy needs assessment is impractical. For example, a health care insurance provider that had been processing claims manually

---

Box 4.1   TECHNOLOGICAL CHANGE READINESS ASSESSMENT TOOL

Using the scale below, please circle the number that best describes attitudes and practices in your organization.

Strongly Disagree	Disagree	Neutral	Agree	Strongly Agree
1	2	3	4	5

1 2 3 4 5   People in this organization readily accept change.

1 2 3 4 5   Past introductions of new technology have gone smoothly.

1 2 3 4 5   Clear business goals are guiding the introduction of the new technology.

1 2 3 4 5   The new technology will improve job quality in our organization.

1 2 3 4 5   The new technology will improve job security.

1 2 3 4 5   People trust upper management to make technology decisions.

1 2 3 4 5   There is good communication between management and employees.

1 2 3 4 5   We have the money needed to invest in new technology.

1 2 3 4 5   Our employees are willing to be trained to work with new technology.

1 2 3 4 5   The physical infrastructure of our workplace can readily accommodate new technology.

Scoring: Total your score and divide by 10.
5 = Strong readiness for change;
4 = Moderate readiness for change—some work must be done to improve areas with lower scores;
3 = Need to do further assessment to determine change readiness;
2 = Not yet ready to engage in change; considerable preparation needed;
1 = Change is likely to fail if implemented before extensive internal work is done.

found that as its business grew, customer service waned. The only way to improve operational efficiency and thus service quality was to introduce new technology—computer workstations and software designed in-house that provided scanning, batching, labeling, indexing, and electronic retrieval capabilities. Such a system promised to improve claim accuracy, processing timeliness, and claim tracking capability, thereby improving service to customers. In this case, an expedited needs assessment was required, thereby permitting the organization to move more quickly to the change readiness assessment phase and determining the best method of implementing this system.

Similarly, a police department in a large metropolitan area charged with the goals of maintaining peace and reducing crime sought to increase arrests by 5% to 10% over a 12-month period and to improve the quality of life for residents. An enhancement to its "911" emergency call and dispatch system became available. This new technology—computers with word recognition software—would monitor all incoming data and color code it according to (a) danger to police, (b) identification of a perpetrator or victim, or (c) recovery of a weapon, illegal drug, or contraband. Citizens phoning the emergency number twice within a short time period would get expedited service, and the codes would enable a more precise police response. The software would also play an important role in providing updated information to officers responding to an emergency call.

In both of these cases, the organizations stood to increase efficiency and responsiveness to citizen-customer needs by adopting the new technology. By expediting the needs analysis process and by performing a variance analysis, these organizations could advance more quickly to the readiness assessment phase of the change process. Readiness assessment is a vital component of the technological change planning process, for even when it appears that technology is good for the organization, there may be employees who do not agree with this judgment. In the case of the police department, dispatchers are likely to be less than enthusiastic about the new 911 technology, fearing added job stress at best and job dislocation at worst. Knowing this prior to implementation is very important so that training and redeployment can be built into the overall technology adoption plan.

Inclusive Needs Assessment

Involving a broad cross-section of stakeholders in the technology planning process helps to promote needs readiness by making needs assessment a collective, engaging experience. This certainly appears to have been the case in the East Detroit, Michigan public school district, where a 70-person Technology Task Force was developed, with representatives from a broad base of the community as well as the schools. Input from the task force shaped a strategic long-range plan and integrated curriculum. The school district hired a director of educational technology to oversee this process and to provide leadership for the instructional technology programs and the technology management process. The subsequent success of the district's technology adoption, use, and educational outcomes was attributed in large part to its inclusive planning process (U.S. Department of Education, 1999).

Another Michigan school district also used an inclusive process to determine whether or not to purchase a computer-based integrated learning system for the teaching of high school math and science. After receiving information about this program from the vendor, the director of secondary education surveyed teachers to determine their need for such a system and then forwarded these specifications to the company selling the software. The software company adjusted the software program to meet teacher needs and agreed to allow schools to pilot test the program for one year, during which time hardware and software problems and incompatibilities were resolved. The teachers involved in the pilot test then became trainers of other teachers.

A second, more systemic example of inclusive needs assessment at the same district was the development of a Technology Inquiry Group to study current and "best practice" pertaining to the integration of instructional technology into the elementary school curriculum, and to make recommendations about a computer-based integrated learning system. This group consisted of one teacher from each elementary school, a representative from the teacher association executive board, principals from each elementary school, a media specialist and clerk, four computer paraprofessionals, a representative from the district technology department, the district director of staff development, and a consultant.

This group developed a framework for the elementary school technology curriculum and highlighted several models for the integration of technology into subject and grade curricula, including models that had been developed by elementary teachers in the district. The inquiry group also recommended that each school building establish a "technology team" to develop a 3-year building technology plan and provide leadership in the acquisition and use of the technology.

Summary

The first step in the technology adoption life cycle is analyzing technology needs and readiness for change. Needs analysis involves identifying the most pressing business and organizational goals, analyzing performance in relation to those goals, identifying the type(s) and amount of technology needed, calculating technology costs and benefits, and developing a plan for evaluating technology performance. Broad goals such as "improved quality" should be broken down into quantifiable components like "fewer defects" or "fewer customer complaints."

Variance analysis is a methodology used in sociotechnical system design to measure deviations from expected performance and to determine causes of the variations. It can help decision makers determine whether technology or organizational variables are accountable for substandard performance. This chapter provided an illustration of the variance analysis technique as applied to a hospital setting.

Organizations adopt technology not only to correct problems but also to pursue new business opportunities. Whatever the motivation, it is best to "shop" for the most appropriate technology with the best price, terms, and service. Performed before technology purchase, a cost-benefit analysis examines intangible as well as tangible costs and benefits. Cost-benefit approaches that use activity-based costing and economic value-added estimation are favored over traditional accounting methods that use direct labor as a basis for allocating overhead expenses to production costs. A seven-step process is recommended for technology cost-benefit justification, using an example from a higher education institution.

After conducting the needs analysis and cost-benefit analysis and justification, an organization should perform an analysis of change readiness. This analysis will help to identify internal obstacles that might hinder technological change, such as negative attitudes, inappropriate organizational structure/levels of hierarchy, poor labor relations and top-down governance, inadequate physical and technical infrastructure, human resources, and financial resources. Methodologies for measuring change readiness are offered in this chapter.

There are times when a lengthy needs assessment is impractical, as in the case of the two examples provided—one from health care and the other from law enforcement. In such situations, the needs assessment should be expedited but not bypassed altogether. It should also be stressed that the involvement of a broad cross-section of stakeholders in the needs assessment process can be very beneficial, as the examples from the public school sector illustrate.

Five

Organizational Barriers to Integrated Change

When planning for the introduction of new technology, managers typically focus most of their energies on the acquisition and installation of the equipment or software. They tend to spend comparatively less time on assessing the fit between the technology and the organization into which it will be introduced. Yet organizational variables can "make or break" technology effectiveness. Identifying and eliminating organizational barriers before bringing the technology online helps to pave the way for technology success.

Identifying Organizational Variables

Macro-Level Organizational Variables

There are numerous organizational variables that affect change processes in any company, public sector agency, educational institution, or hospital. They may be classified as either "macro-level" variables that affect the entire institution, or "micro-level" variables that pertain to individual employees in specific ways. Figure 5.1 depicts both macro (outer ring) and micro (inner circle) variables common to any organization.

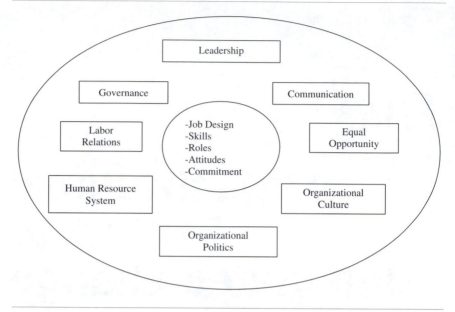

Figure 5.1   Macro and Micro-Level Organizational Variables

At the macro-level, *organizational structure* refers to the layout of an organization's governing executives, functional departments and units, and the reporting relationships between them. Organizational structure is often depicted in the form of an organizational chart. Many factors and philosophies can influence organizational structure. An organization may be "tall" with many layers of hierarchy from top to bottom, or "flat" with virtually no middle management and a greater "span of control" (number of people reporting to a single manager) from top to bottom (Northcraft & Neale, 1990, pp. 678–679). Organizations seeking to push governance down to frontline employees or those that want nimble, responsive management systems typically opt for flatter organizational structures. Organizational size and complexity can influence the structure chosen; large organizations are often, but not necessarily, more bureaucratic and decentralized than smaller ones.

Hierarchy notwithstanding, there are also different ways to organize departments or units. They may be structured in the following ways:

1. Functional specialization (e.g., placing all engineers working on instrument panel design in one group regardless of the vehicle they are working on)

2. Product or service (e.g., self-contained product/service-focused units or teams that have enough dedicated functional specialists to

produce a product or render a service, as in the case of Amcar described in Chapter 1)

3. Matrix (a combination of the functional and product/service models in which functional and product/service groups exist and report to two managers)

4. Geography (organization of a company, agency, or university by geographic location, with separate and duplicative managerial structures for each region, city, etc.)

5. Network (organizations use information technology and other advancements to operate in tandem with supplier and/or other organizations to produce a product or offer a service). (Hellriegel, Slocum, & Woodman, 1989, pp. 370–379; Robbins, 1991, p. 328).

Organizational structure is important because the adoption of new technology may require a change in personnel deployment or reporting relationships to optimize its effectiveness. For example, a university that is trying to encourage faculty to become more computer proficient would do well to place computer information systems specialists in each college or across several departments instead of housing all of them in a single support unit. An organization may adopt different forms for certain phases of the technology life cycle (e.g., using a matrix structure for technology/product research and development), or may opt for a hybrid approach, which uses one or more organizational forms (Gattiker & Ulhoi, 1999).

Closely related to organizational structure is *governance*—the formal patterns of decision-making authority. Theoretically, institutions with flatter management structures push decision-making downward, though this is not a given, for autocratic leadership can still occur with few hierarchical levels. Still, organizations that are committed to the concept of strategic partnership must remove enough of the layers of authority to allow decisions to percolate up from the bottom.

Shared governance requires effective *leadership* at the highest level of the organization. In an analysis of why change efforts fail, Kotter (1995) finds that top management must communicate a clear and compelling vision and "walk the talk" by modeling the practices that they promulgate verbally. Oden (1997) argues that visionary leaders are successful only to the extent that they can "inspire others" to endorse the program and "touch the hearts of the employees." What neither of these authors state, however, is that in a strategic partnership approach, the articulation of vision must reflect the interests of employees, not only top management. Where a local union is present, its leadership must also be visionary—able to see beyond immediate needs with a view toward long-range objectives.

Effective leadership at the top and effective governance at the bottom of the organization require ongoing formal *communication* that flows from top to bottom and back up to top. Although memoranda, electronic mail, posted notices, and newsletter articles are better than no communication, face-to-face meetings are by far the most effective form because there is an opportunity for two-way interaction and clarification. Some organizations hold large-group meetings on a quarterly basis to share performance results or new directions. Local union leaders should be invited to speak about partnership initiatives or comment on performance and new opportunities. Supplementing organization-wide meetings with monthly small-group meetings within departments or units is one of the best ways to encourage bottom-up information sharing.

Labor relations refers to all dimensions of the labor-management relationship. In unionized settings, this includes the collective bargaining agreement negotiated between the parties, grievances that arise in the course of administering that agreement, and collaborative efforts that extend beyond the requirements of the contract. A good labor-management relationship is characterized by an expansive collective bargaining agreement, strong and visionary local leadership (union and management), a low grievance rate, labor-management trust and mutual respect, the free exchange of information, and advance consultation or joint determination of workplace change. As stated in Chapter 2, a poor labor-management relationship can serve as a significant barrier to technological change and improved performance.

Equal opportunity is the extent to which all employees have fair and equal chances for retention and advancement, regardless of gender, race, age, sexual orientation, and all other personal attributes unrelated to job performance. If technology is introduced into a workplace that already discriminates against women by limiting the jobs they have access to, the new technology is likely to be used in ways that perpetuate rather than eliminate that discrimination (Haddad, 1987; Wajcman, 1991).

Because many new technologies have reduced requirements of physical strength on the job, there is a golden opportunity to adopt technologies that open fresh job opportunities to women. The effect on gender and on all workforce groups should certainly be taken into account when "shopping" for new technology. When one local police department adopted a new, lightweight pistol, it had not considered the fact that female officers would find its strong kickback dangerous, thereby placing them in potential jeopardy during shooting incidents.

The *human resource system* should work in tandem with the planned technological change. Because the technology may require new work arrangements (e.g., teams), skills, and even new job classifications, human resource managers must be consulted early in the planning process so that training, compensation incentives, and other supportive elements can be put in place. Of course, a partnership approach assumes that union representatives are invited to work with human resource managers in the formulation of pay and performance and reward strategies.

The "Amcar" Corporation discussed in Chapter 1 crafted several human resource practices to support the use of concurrent engineering philosophy and product-focused team structure at its engineering center. One practice was a performance appraisal system that rewarded teamwork by evaluating skill and behavior, not just results. The evaluation process also included input from subordinates, peers, and customers. A second practice was the development of a training matrix that identified all mandatory (e.g., health and safety) and optional training in the company. Attainment of training goals was another part of the employee appraisal system. Still another practice was to post job openings on a corporate-wide basis to encourage cross-functional job mobility (Haddad, 1996a).

Organizational culture and *organizational politics* work at an informal level to either support or thwart change activities. Oden (1997) has gone so far as to state, "The many reasons cited for the failure of organizational behavior change efforts can be reduced to one sentence: *The culture of the organization remained unchanged*" (p. 50). Organizational culture generally refers to shared beliefs, values, expectations, attitudes, norms philosophies, and climate (Kilman, Saxton, & Serpa's work as cited in Hellriegel et al., 1989). Manifestations of organizational culture include particular group behavior, language, attachment to artifacts, and emotion (Hellriegel et al., 1989; Schein, 1985). A "shop floor" culture that is distrustful of technology and an engineering culture that deifies it may have a difficult time blending as partners in a cooperative team-based relationship without incentives for shedding old beliefs (Haddad, 1996c).

Organizational politics has been defined by Pfeffer (as cited in Hellriegel et al., 1989, p. 436) as "actions by individuals or groups to acquire, develop, and use power and other resources in order to obtain preferred outcomes when there is uncertainty or disagreement about choices." Knights and Murray (1994) note that organizational politics center around the struggle of individuals and groups to achieve and maintain "material and symbolic security" (p. 30). The introduction of new technology can unwittingly contribute to solidification or conversely disruption of informal power bases among certain populations or individuals within an organization. A nonmanagerial employee with great computer proficiency may be transformed from a person with no influence to someone with considerable informal power once the department becomes computerized.

Knights and Murray (1994) argue that organizational politics are "central to the development and deployment of information technology" (p. 28). They contend that organizational politics influence and are influenced by factors such as the organizational hierarchy, rules, and division of labor; technological expertise; sociopolitical inequalities based on gender, race, class, and ownership of capital; and individual levels of security.

Gash (1987) illustrates the technology and politics link from a different perspective. After studying the political dimensions of microcomputers, she concludes that they are not merely "technical tools for accomplishing tasks" but also "political tools" that can alter "the distribution of power in organizations" (p. 151). She further argues that access to computers and the information they generate is a dimension of organizational power. Although computers are by no means the sole source of organizational power and authority, the contribution that they and other technology make to the alteration of power relationships needs to be anticipated prior to technology adoption.

Micro-Level Organizational Variables

At the level of the individual, *job design*—the constellation of job tasks, duties, and responsibilities and the characteristics of the job (e.g., safety, degree of autonomy)—are affected by technological change. Technology has the potential to make jobs safer (e.g., robotic paint spraying in automotive factories that had previously exposed workers to those fumes), more ergonomic (e.g., adjustable equipment at work stations), more skilled (e.g., technologies that draw on employees' cognitive and problem-solving abilities), and more interesting (e.g., greater task variation).

Conversely, the application of technology to jobs can result in high stress (where work becomes more demanding and faster paced), health problems (e.g., eye, wrist, and back strain from extended computer use), electronic monitoring of work performance, and greater isolation (e.g., "telework"—working remotely). Adverse effects on jobs will inevitably result in adverse effects on technology performance. Employees will justifiably resist working with the technology, and when they do, it will not perform to its highest potential.

Job design can be measured by observation, interview, and survey. The ModArt instrument developed by this author measures task autonomy, work pace, and control over such, stress, safety, ergonomics, and training adequacy. Another instrument is the Job Diagnostic Survey (JDS) developed by Hackman and Oldham (1974). The job dimensions measured by the JDS are skill variety, task significance, autonomy, job feedback, and dealings with others. There are advantages to using a standardized instrument developed by researchers or consultants insofar as statistical reliability will have been tested. Still, even using interviews and observation to ascertain job design dimensions in advance of technology introduction is better than ignoring the need for a pretechnology assessment.

It is also useful to assess *job skills* prior to bringing new technology on line. "Skill" is a multidimensional construct. It can refer to manual motor ability (e.g., the ability to physically and precisely manipulate tools and equipment), knowledge (e.g., understanding key concepts pertinent to the job or field, problem-solving ability, and creativity), autonomy (judgment and discretion in planning and performing work), and control—independence and freedom from significant external control or rigid structure (Haddad, 1988). Spenner (1990) argues that skill is socially constructed, incorporating two broad dimensions: (a) "substantive complexity" defined as the "level, scope and integration of mental, manipulative, and interpersonal tasks in a job," and (b) "autonomy-control"—the "discretion or leeway available in a job to control the content, manner and speed in which tasks are done," not to be equated with formal authority (pp. 402–403).

In measuring skill, three primary methods are used: testing (particularly of technical and knowledge skills), job task analysis by trained experts, and employee self-reporting via surveys. Although some may argue that the latter method is biased, Spenner (1990) believes that employees "are fairly accurate perceivers and reporters of their immediate job situation" (p. 416).

The reasons for measuring job skill in advance of new technology's arrival are twofold. One is to determine whether employees have the skills needed to manipulate, monitor, and maintain the new equipment or software. Skills assessment can serve as the basis of training content. A second reason for advance skill measurement is to provide a baseline against which subsequent performance can be compared. This can help the individual and the organization determine whether specific skill dimensions have been upgraded or downgraded or replaced with other skill sets as a result of the new technology. If downgrading has occurred, this would be cause for concern and remedial action with respect to technology use. It is not wise to spend money on new technology only to have it result in jobs that are more boring, stressful, and less reliant on worker judgment and knowledge.

Work *roles* are "clusters of tasks that others expect a person to perform in doing a job" (Hellriegel et al., 1989, p. 459). Role conflict can occur when changes in the workplace, such as restructuring and the introduction of new technology, cause a redefinition of a work role, and the affected employee does not adjust to the new expectations.

Although much attention is focused on the notion of recalcitrant employees or "Luddites" following the introduction of new technology and work reorganization, it may well be frontline supervisors who experience the greatest role conflict. This is especially true when they have been left out of decisions about the change, when they are expected to forego their role as authority enforcers and become "coaches" and facilitators in flatter organizations, and when they are as unfamiliar with the technology as the employees whom they supervise, yet responsible for the smooth operation of the work process.

Paying close attention to preexisting work roles and changes that may be required to accommodate the envisioned strategic innovations—technological and organizational—is the first necessary step. Discussions with affected employees about anticipated role changes and solicitation of input on alternatives is the second step in ensuring smooth role transition. Third, training may be needed. Finally, a revamping of the performance appraisal and reward system will be needed, so that expected roles are properly recognized. Greater role conflict will occur if after the redefinition and training of supervisors, for example, they are still rewarded on the basis of how well they enforce managerial authority.

Employee *attitudes* and *commitment* to the organization are closely related. Some commonly measured attitudes are the following:

1. Job satisfaction

2. Job involvement

3. Intention to seek a new job

4. Likelihood of finding a comparable job with another employer

5. Desire to seek a new job within the same organization

6. Internal work motivation

7. Degree of job effort

8. Task quality (job challenge, meaning, and responsibility)

9. Organizational involvement

10. Compensation satisfaction. (Cammann, Fichman, Jenkins, & Klesh, 1983)

Other attitudinal measures , such as those appearing in the ModArt survey designed by this author, assess employee attitudes toward the following:

1. Need for modernization (technology and work reorganization)

2. Satisfaction with job security

3. Climate of recognition and appreciation of employees

4. Satisfaction with respect and fair treatment

5. Job satisfaction

6. Commitment

7. Satisfaction with managerial support and guidance

8. Receptivity of employees to technological change

9. Quality of the labor-management relationship

No matter which survey instrument is used, there is value in measuring employee attitudes about new technology and workplace management issues in general before introducing technological change. Because technology is often brought online in piecemeal fashion rather than all at once, an employee attitude assessment can reveal which units might be more receptive to it than others. Measuring attitudes through an anonymous written survey (in which employees list only their job classification and unit/department) is the best way to gauge attitudes, provided that a representative and sizable sample of employees participates and responds to the survey. Administering it during working hours will ensure the highest rates of participation, which should always be voluntary, and union representatives (or employee representatives in nonunion workplaces) should be involved in designing/reviewing the instrument, endorsing its administration, and interpretation of the results.

What Influences Attitudes Toward New Technology?

Employee attitudes toward their jobs and their employer are influenced by a myriad of factors including job structure, management practices, and the match between personal needs and job realities. Employee attitudes toward new technology may be somewhat influenced by inherent comfort level with new challenges or other personal factors. However, managerial practice plays a large role in shaping the views of employees toward technological change, as the Brownvale case illustrates.

Brownvale Plant Revisited

The author conducted survey and interview research at the Brownvale plant described in Chapter 1 to determine which organizational and technological factors best explained employee attitudes toward new technology (Haddad, 1996d). The factors studied were the following:

1. *Level of complexity of the technology* used on the job (an automated storage and retrieval system was labeled a "complex" technological system requiring major job restructuring, compared to a "simple" stand-alone computer-controlled assembly stand; some of the employees used no new technology)

2. *Training* in the use of the new technology

3. *Duration* of new technology use

4. *Advance notification* of the new technology's introduction into their jobs

5. The *job position* held in the organization (e.g., managerial, technical, skilled trades, or production workers)

6. *Leadership in one of the two unions* representing employees at the plant

Employee attitudes toward new technology were defined as technology's reported effect on work monitoring, ease of work, speed of work, quality, variety and challenge, stress, job security, and job safety.

It was hypothesized that:

H1. Users of complex technology would have less favorable attitudes toward the technology than those working with simple or no technology, because the complex technology altered job tasks substantially and required new learning.

H2. Employees who were given training in preparation for the technology would have more positive attitudes toward technology than those who were not offered training.

H3. Employees who had worked with either of the two technology types for more than two years would feel more positively toward new technology than those who had worked with the technology for a shorter period.

H4. Advance notification would positively affect employee attitudes toward the new technology.

H5. Job position would prove to be a significant predictor of attitudes toward new technology.

H6. Leadership in a local union affects employee attitudes toward new technology.

Hypotheses 3, 4, and 5 were supported statistically (based on regression analysis). The fact that duration of technology use predicted attitudes toward new technology suggests that employee attitudes are likely to improve as the "learning curve" rises with extended use. The finding that advance notification of technology introduction is a predictor of positive attitudes toward new technology supports a central contention of this book—that open and participative change leads to better results than closed, top-down decision-making processes.

The emergence of job position as a significant predictor of attitudes toward technology led to the use of an additional statistical test (analysis of variance) to determine *which* of the four categories of employees had the most positive attitudes toward new technology. The results were somewhat surprising. The rank order from most to least positive was (a) managers, (b) skilled trades employees, (c) technical employees, and (d) production employees. Technicians, who bore the greatest responsibility for bringing the new technology online and error free, had less positive feelings about it than skilled trades employees who participated in its installation. Thus, although preexisting job roles can influence employee attitudes toward new technology (managers had more access to information and were more positive about it than production employees), the very process of implementation also plays a role in determining employee receptivity to technological change.

The fact that training did not emerge as a significant predictor of employee attitudes toward new technology does not mean that training is not important. To the contrary, training is significant enough that Chapter 7 in this volume is entirely devoted to it. Rather, this finding was more a function of the manner in which training was conducted—too little and too late (only two employees reported receiving training *before* the technology was brought online). Moreover, "in an environment in which workplace learning is impeded by hierarchical management practices and narrowly defined job tasks, training alone cannot impart the knowledge required to operate new technologies effectively" (Haddad, 1996d, p. 158). When roles and relationships on the factory floor limit worker judgment and discretion, training is not likely to have an optimal impact on employee problem-solving ability (Hirschhorn, 1989, p. 37).

Union leadership also did not play a role in predicting employee attitudes toward new technology. Although it may be popular to assume that union leaders necessarily oppose the introduction of new technology for short-sighted protectionist reasons, that myth is dispelled by this study. In fact, interviews with union leaders at Brownvale revealed that they sought early, more extensive input in the technology implementation process than they were actually given. Union leaders do, of course, care about the impact of technology on the jobs and working conditions of their members, and their input should be welcomed by management because it is likely to lead to more enriched jobs—an outcome consistent with a high-performance workplace.

This case study demonstrates that the very process of adopting and implementing technological change has a significant impact on employee attitudes toward the new technology—regardless of the complexity of the technology introduced. Advance notification and the ability to exert some control over the implementation process can serve as a basis for greater worker receptivity to new technology's arrival.

Overcoming Resistance to Change

No matter how well management plans for the introduction of technology and assesses the organizational factors described in this chapter, there are bound to be employees—managerial and nonmanagerial—who resist any change in their job routine. Noori (1990, p. 276), citing Kotter and Schlesinger, offers a continuum of solutions that organizations can employ to deal with employee resistance to change. Their solutions range from education, communication, participation and involvement to manipulation, cooptation, and coercion. These authors acknowledge the drawbacks associated with the latter negative strategies, but they also note that these strategies are quick and inexpensive compared to the former methods.

It is indeed true that education, communication, and participation are time consuming and more costly in the short run. But it is folly to presume that coercion is without cost. Employees rightly resist coercion and manipulation, whether directly by filing a grievance that can delay the benefits of change, or indirectly by seeking work elsewhere or engaging in sabotage. It is certainly more costly to recruit and train new employees than to bring existing employees along cooperatively.

Still, in situations where poor supervision or narrowly defined jobs have existed for years, employee morale may be so low that it is impossible to dive head first into the pool of radical change. A slower approach is needed—one driven by new or reinvigorated leadership that employs an open process of communication and that seeks employee and union input in the definition of the problem and the formulation of the solution.

Once the change has been outlined, agreed to, and implemented, there may be some employees and managers who continue to be resistors. If they cannot be brought along and encouraged through training, rewards, and coaching, it may be best to develop voluntary termination or early retirement incentives. Although there will always be some employees who oppose change in any form, their numbers and influence are reduced when the transition process has been managed in a strategic, participative, and open manner. Genuine involvement and recognition are the best antidotes to worker alienation, and alienation is one of the primary sources of recalcitrance. Fear is another source, but it also can be overcome through training and assurances of job security for those who are willing to give their best effort.

In the end, organizational factors can serve either to smooth the process of implementing new technology, or conversely, can act as major obstacles along the way. By being aware of and addressing the macro and micro-level organizational variables described in this chapter, those directing the change process will have the greatest chance of success as they proceed forward in a slow and consultative fashion. Ignoring organizational factors and employee feelings will almost guarantee a rocky start-up and poor results.

Summary

Organizational barriers to technological change can thwart successful implementation and use of new technology. These barriers can be found at the macro (organizational) or micro (worker) level. Potential barriers at the organizational level include organizational structure and hierarchy, governance, leadership, communication, labor relations, equal opportunity, human resource practices, organizational culture, and organizational politics. Potential barriers at the worker level include job design, job skill, work roles, and employee attitudes.

Managerial practice has a great deal of influence over employee attitudes toward technological change. Research conducted by the author at the Brownvale plant demonstrates that advance notification, job position, and the duration of new technology use affect employee attitudes toward the new technology. Job position results from this study particularly showed that those categories of employees who had the greatest control over the implementation process had more positive attitudes toward the technology than those who did not. The study also confirms that early communication about technology's impending arrival can help to improve employee receptivity to it. Yet it is still common management practice to withhold notification until the point of installation. An important lesson is that communication and participation will generally ensure greater receptivity to technological change.

Six

Designing and Implementing Strategic Change

Two types of design are important to the technology management process—the design of technology itself and the design of the technological change process. A central thesis of this chapter is that strategy and participation should guide each of these design processes.

The need for a well-designed implementation process is illustrated by the Brownvale case (discussed in Chapter 5), which demonstrated that employee attitudes toward new technology are influenced by the process of change. All too often, new technology introduction is guided by the "mushroom theory of management"—keep employees in the dark, throw a bit of manure on them, and hope that they grow. Long before Amcar Corporation reorganized and adopted a concurrent engineering philosophy (discussed in Chapter 1), an electrician reported that he had been called into work on a Sunday to install a new robotic system. Realizing that employees were paid "double time" wages for Sunday work, I asked him why he had been deployed on that day. His reply was that management wanted the new system in place to greet assemblers reporting to work on Monday morning. Unfortunately, this scenario is all too common in workplaces. In many an organization, employees first learn of new technology's impending arrival when the cartons appear on the loading dock.

Social Constructivism and Technology Design

There are two primary philosophies about what influences the design and development of technology. According to the rational-objectivist view, technology emerges from objective, empirical scientific discovery and rational, logical thought processes, which are largely independent of societal influences (Volti, 1995, pp. 11–14). As Volti (1995) has noted, rational objectivists tend to see nature as something to be conquered and generally seek to "dominate their world" (p. 13). A related view—that technology leads and society follows—is referred to as "technological determinism" (Pacey, 1983, p. 24).

The second philosophy is known as social constructivism or social constructionism. Thomas Kuhn described this approach in his classic treatise, *The Structure of Scientific Revolutions*. Essentially, proponents of this view argue that there is no such thing as objective science, because subjective influences such as social beliefs and values influence seemingly rational thought (Pool, 1997, pp. 12–13). Pacey (1983) describes this as the cultural dimension of technology, although he further argues that there are also organizational influences on technology practice (pp. 4–6). Thus, even scientific discoveries, and certainly technological ones, can be socially constructed or influenced. In fact, Webster (1991) goes so far as to assert that "the traditional view that science and technology are 'neutral,' uninfluenced by wider social processes, can no longer be sustained" (p. 5). These social processes may be cultural, organizational, or political.

Gender bias can be one such social influence on technology design. The early, nonadjustable shoulder harnesses in cars, some would argue, were designed with male and not female passengers in mind. The same was true of early bulletproof vests for police officers, which did not properly fit most female members of law enforcement agencies. Morgall (1993), among others, contends that the reason for this is that women are "not represented proportionally" in the technology research and development process (p. 3). Even with their numbers increasing, it is thought that women scientists who are oriented toward cooperation often find themselves at odds with a highly competitive and combative work environment (Morse, 1995). Social constructivists put forth a compelling argument that technology design is influenced by social factors.

Participative Technology Design

Theory and Practice: United States and Europe

In March 1989 a conference titled, "Designing for Technological Change: People in the Process," was sponsored by the National Academy of Engineering and the National Research Council's Commission on Behavioral and Social Sciences and Education (National Research Council, 1991). Presenters from service, health care, telecommunications, nonprofit, and manufacturing sectors shared examples of employee involvement in technology and work redesign. The cases varied in the degree of employee and union influence at the decision-making stage, but the conference was significant nonetheless in its recognition of the need for "people" involvement in the design of change.

In general, though, while isolated examples of worker-union involvement in technology systems design do exist, the preponderance of the engineering literature on system design excludes any mention of skill-based properties or worker involvement in design (Salzman, 1990). One U.S. case study presented by Salzman (1990) illustrates the benefits of worker and union involvement in technology design. This occurred at a large aerospace company's machining shop, which was redesigned, with the involvement of machinists, into work cells. The machinists' suggestions about the types of machines needed, selection of vendors, and the layout of the cells resulted in great operational efficiency and improved safety. Moreover, their involvement in system design encouraged them to develop cross-discipline job knowledge and in some cases to advance their own formal education. The machinists also benefited financially from a postimplementation suggestion system that encouraged their continued involvement in process improvement (Salzman, 1990).

Some European countries have had more of a tradition of participatory work and technology design, as demonstrated by the following examples. Still, even in these countries, participatory design is the exception rather than the norm (Latniak, 1995).

Scandinavia

Norway's Industrial Democracy Program dating back to the 1960s (Elden et al., 1982) and its 1977 Work Environment Act, and Sweden's 1976 Co-determination at Work Act (ILO, 1981, cited in Haddad, 1984) offered a legal and policy context for labor participation in technology design. Although sometimes this participation took place "after the fact"—once key decisions about system design and implementation had been made by management, examples of proactive union involvement could be found in both countries (Early & Witt, 1982; Schneider, 1983). One such well-publicized example was Sweden's UTOPIA project in which graphics workers' unions in the newspaper industry, with assistance from researchers at the Swedish Center for Working Life, developed skill-based software systems that met union criteria for "quality work and quality products" (Bodker et al., 1987, cited in Benders, de Haan, & Bennett, 1995; Schneider, 1983, p. 19).

Germany

Germany, too, has some history of worker participation in *technikgestaltung*—the shaping of technology, from design and development to implementation and use (Latniak, 1995). The enterprise-level works councils established under German codetermination law (which provides a formal mechanism for union cogovernance on certain issues) can in theory influence technology decisions before implementation. But worker and union influence in technology design requires management commitment to an "anthropocentric" approach—one in which "blue collar work expertise" is valued and used (Wobbe, 1995).

Toward this end, researchers at centers such as the Institute for Work and Technology in Northrhine-Westphalia, particularly its Department of Production Systems, serve as designers and consultants to unions and workers seeking human-centered, skill-promoting technologies. These researchers believe that to have a "learning organization," the information technology to be used therein must be "designed as tools to support the accomplishment of individual working tasks and as media for cooperation and communication" (Banke, Brödner, González, & Oehike, 1977, p. 7).

One of the projects of this Institute was the design of a new work-oriented programming (WOP) technique for numerically controlled (NC) machine tools that can be programmed by skilled workers themselves. The result has been that "skilled workers make use of their manufacturing knowledge, their planning capabilities, and their situational knowledge about the states of machines and tools in order to efficiently produce correct and optimize NC programs" (Banke et al., 1977, p. 25). There were fewer programming errors than when remote programmers had done this work, and for the skilled trades employees "existing skills and knowledge are activated and maintained rather than being replaced through objectification in software" (Banke et al., 1977, p. 25).

European researchers of similar mind have also come together transnationally, with support from the European Union, to exchange dialogue and collaborate at events such as the meetings of Forecasting and Assessment in the Field of Science and Technology (FAST). One cross-national project stemming from this interaction was ESPRIT 1217, a collaborative effort of British, Danish, and German researchers to develop a human-centered Computer Integrated Manufacturing (CIM) system (Banke et al., 1977).

United Kingdom

In the United Kingdom, Howard Rosenbrock, former Professor of Control Engineering at the University of Manchester Institute of Science and Technology (UMIST), was a strident advocate for the design of machines that "accept" and "collaborate" with worker skill and that are "subordinate to people" (Rosenbrock, 1983). He argued that instead of developing "expert systems" in which employees are rendered obsolete once their knowledge becomes codified and embedded in the technology, computers should assist skilled humans in diagnosing problems (Rosenbrock, 1983). Among the projects he led was human-centered software development for a computer numerically controlled lathe (Corbett, 1990, p. 122).

The examples from all of these countries illustrate the value-added role of employees and their unions in designing new technologies and work systems.

Case Study: From the U.S. Health Care Industry

A case study from the U.S. health care sector demonstrates the benefit of earlier and more extensive employee and union involvement in technology design. The University of Wisconsin Hospital and Clinics Nursing Administration and the United Professionals for Quality Health Care (affiliated with Local 1199 of the Service Employees International Union) along with research and technical assistance from a professor at the University's School for Workers, came together at the union's initiation to develop a nursing information system. The union president and executive director, cognizant of the labor-displacing implications of technological change, approached hospital management with the idea of collaboratively developing technology that used skilled nurses to improve health care delivery (Alvin, Roberts, Schultz, Trimborn, & Emspak, 1998).

After agreeing on a target project and with funding from the Federal Mediation and Conciliation Service and matching money from the University of Wisconsin Hospital and Clinics, the parties worked for a 2-year period on the design of a new information system. They established a Nursing Information System Development Group (NISDG), which included two subcommittees: (a) Design Criteria, which focused on the design features and specifications of the intended system, and (b) Public Relations, to provide information to the general body of nurses and to the public at-large.

The development group had already concluded that the existing clinical information system was cumbersome, time-consuming, and not designed to support the work of nurses, in large part because the system was developed by information systems staff, not end users. These developers knew that a new system needed to (a) provide management and nurses with needed and easily accessible patient information, (b) foster communication and coordination across the various levels of health care providers (e.g., nursing staff, emergency personnel, etc.), and (c) support the unique needs of nursing without intruding on or eliminating face-to-face contact between nurses and patients. The value statement drafted by the Design Group was as follows:

> We are committed to nursing as a profession and believe that nursing is and should remain an integral part of the health care delivery system. Developing technology to enhance our contributions to that system will increase our efficiency and effectiveness, and positively impact our ability to maintain our unique role in the delivery system. (Alvin et al., 1998)

The design specifications of the information system were intended to standardize advice to patients and ensure that they understood that advice, improve networking among all the caregivers responsible for a given patient (e.g., lab, X-ray, physical therapy, nurse-to-nurse, etc.), access patient's current medical record and previous history, streamline documentation and decrease multiple entry of information and paper-work, provide information for discharge planning and communications with outside facilities, and be user-friendly, portable and voice activated.

In performing its research and design work, the development committee, through a process of consensus decision making, performed the following activities:

- Mapped information flow and diagramed causes and effects pertaining to patient care in a variety of settings (e.g., clinics, inpatient units, surgical services, etc.)
- Led seven focus group discussions with staff nurses to ensure accuracy of mapping and to gather input on information system priorities
- Developed an outline of design criteria for a nursing clinical information system
- Met with information system consultants to discuss design criteria
- Reviewed and modified the design specifications report of the information system consultants
- Sponsored a technology fair to review various technologies available
- Shared preliminary findings with the director of information systems and medical director of information systems
- Presented the design specifications to the hospital and clinics Information System Strategic Planning Group (senior managers and physicians) who endorsed the plan
- Met with the hospital and clinics superintendent and gained his support for the design specifications and implementation plan

- Integrated the nursing care information systems (IS) plan into the hospital IS strategic plan
- Dedicated hospital-clinics' IS staff to work with the Nursing Information System Development Group (Alvin et al., 1998)

Although a change in local union leadership threatened to derail the project, it went forward after extended discussions persuaded the new leaders that NISDG was not undercutting the union's work, and that the resulting information system would benefit all nurses. In the end, a full-time position was created for a nurse to work with the university hospital and clinics' IS department to fine tune the newly developed information system. In addition, the NISDG, which continued to function after the implementation of the nursing information system, was called on to evaluate plans for other new technologies that were under consideration for adoption, including a nurse pocket pager system, laser printer placement in hospital units, a computerized central services catalogue for ordering patient supplies, and placement of networked personal computer (PC) workstations on inpatient hospital units. The NISDG also provided input on the development of training plans for nurses, physicians, and other users.

The Importance of "Skilled Know-How"

The nurses in the University of Wisconsin Hospital case study were able to make valuable contributions to the design of a computer information system, just as machinists in the German and U.S. examples were able to participate in the programming of NC machine tools. These contributions are a function of their "skilled know-how" and experiential learning. Drawing from the teachings of Aristotle, Benner (2001) makes a distinction in her explanation of nurse practitioner skills between "techne"—the application of rational principles of operation and "phronesis"—which requires "character development" and the ability to deal with unpredictable events (p. 60). Although the former aspect of skill is derived from formal study, the "thinking in action and reasoning in transition" that make up phronesis is learned on the job, for it involves "changes in the practitioner's understanding of the clinical situation" and changes "in the patient's condition or concerns" (p. 61). Skilled know-how is neither static nor predictable, for possible outcomes are determined by "emotional attunement, relationship, and skilled action" (Benner, 2000, p. 51).

Not only nurses, but all categories of skilled employees possess skilled know-how. Teachers use skilled know-how when they interact with students who have different learning styles. Law enforcement officers use it when they engage in community policing or interview a suspect. Skilled trades employees use it when they determine how to approach a given task and evaluate the work that has been done. According to Kusterer (1978), it could be argued that all jobs involve skilled know-how, even those that are commonly categorized as "unskilled." In any case, skilled know-how and experiential learning, along with formal technical expertise, serve as the knowledge basis for worker participation in technology design. The challenge facing organizations is the need to transform individual knowledge into organizational learning. The concept of organizational learning will be discussed more fully in Chapter 7.

Prerequisites to Participatory Design

The first prerequisite to participatory technology design in unionized settings (the same principles apply to employees in nonunion enterprises) is management's commitment to regularly sharing information with the union about business strategy and perceived technology needs. Unions are often relegated to after-the-fact participation, because "the union is rarely able to get information about forthcoming systems early enough to actually suggest alternatives to [management]" (Schneider, 1983). This is consistent with survey findings of this author that were presented in Chapter 2 of this volume. When asked how often they were able to take a proactive role in modernization activities at plants they represent, only 17% of responding union leaders replied "very often" or "always," and they cited information sharing and communication between management, union, and shop floor employees and establishment of joint modernization committees as the greatest needed enablers of proactive participation.

The second prerequisite to participatory design is union strategy (see Figure 6.1). In the University of Wisconsin hospital-clinics example, the nurses and their local union leaders led the process of change. They were able to play such a role and approach management with the need for a new information system, because they had a vision of what a new system would do to improve patient care and nursing practice.

A third and equally important prerequisite to participatory design is union access to technical expertise. The University of Wisconsin nurses were assisted by a labor studies professor who helped them find the funding needed to advance their collaborative project. Both parties also benefited from their engagement of information systems specialists who developed the software design specifications with input from the nursing development group. The Swedish graphic workers' union involved in the aforementioned UTOPIA project engaged the technical expertise of researchers at the Swedish Center for Working Life. And the German

Figure 6.1   Prerequisites to Participatory Technology Design

machinists who were involved in the WOP project were assisted by researchers at the Institute for Work and Technology's Department of Production Systems. This union-university/research institute collaboration allows unions to have an independent source of technical expertise, thereby enabling them to participate as equals with their management partners. Equal participation and commitment lead to lasting results.

Technology Implementation Design

As stated at the beginning of this chapter, it is not only technology design but also the design of the implementation process itself that must be planned in advance of technology's introduction. An implementation process that is jointly designed and representative of the workforce will go a long way in smoothing problems with installation, start-up, and continued technology use.

Multilevel Team Structure and Function

A suggested model for structuring teams at different levels is depicted in Figure 6.2. The joint steering committee (first mentioned in Chapter 3) is the committee responsible for setting forth the strategic vision, goals, and parameters of the technological change. It is this group that ensures integration of business and technology strategy, directs the needs assessment and cost analysis, and establishes an overall plan for technology introduction and ongoing evaluation. The steering committee should consist of top-level managers who have authority and access to the organization's strategy and resources, and managers from key constituent groups (e.g., human resources, information systems, etc.). On the union side, it should include top local officers, and representatives of the bargaining council, shop steward structure, and standing committees. In a manufacturing plant, the composition of the steering committee might be as follows:

Management	Union
Plant manager	Local union president
Human resource manager	Vice president
Information systems manager	Secretary
Engineering manager	Bargaining committee chair
Quality control manager	Chief steward
Training manager	Education committee chair

For a school's steering committee, the principal would substitute for the plant manager, and representatives of appropriate grade levels and curriculum committees would serve in place of some of the other slots listed above. In the University of Wisconsin Hospital and Clinics example, the NISDG served as the steering committee.

Members of the steering committee should be selected for strategic reasons and to ensure that the committee has the needed authority and skill mix to lead the change. It is also the role of the steering committee to keep any higher-level management "in the loop" to ensure their continued support for the project. In a school district, for instance, this executive level would include the superintendent and school board members on the management side, and the representative and regional leaders from the state teachers' association on the union side.

The steering committee should charter working committees at the intermediate level, consisting of appointed members that are approved by both parties. At least one steering committee member should serve on these task-specific committees. Figure 6.2 presents one possible configuration that includes a survey committee to assess employee and management technology needs, a cost-benefit committee to analyze ability to purchase the technology and methods of justifying its costs, and a technical design committee to work with information systems/engineering specialists to develop technical specifications for the software and hardware to be developed or purchased. Other possible committees would be a training committee, a health and safety site preparation and maintenance committee, and a publicity and public relations committee. The precise

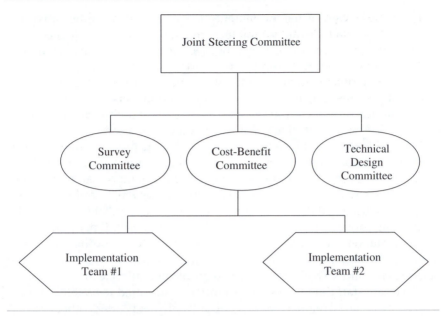

Figure 6.2   Levels of Technological Change Committees

number and composition of these committees will depend on the specific needs and structure of the organization.

Implementation teams operate at the department or unit level, or on a cross-departmental basis if the technology project involves more than one area. It is suggested that the new technology be pilot-tested in one or two areas rather than rolled out across the entire organization all at once. Selection of departments/units should be based on these factors:

1. Strategic business needs

2. The receptivity of employees (frontline users and management) to the proposed technological change (based on the results of a survey, focus groups, or other readiness assessment methods)

3. Technical competency and trainability of employees

Bancroft (1992) adds that although selection criteria can include "geography, function, or interest," pilot approaches to technology implementation "work best when the target group is a small, cohesive department that operates largely independently of others" (p. 191).

The composition of the implementation team will vary, but a typical group would include approximately five operations employees, two supervisors, one technical expert (engineering or systems management), and one quality control technician. Normally the steering committee identifies potential team members with the needed experience, functional role, and peer respect, and approaches them about serving on the implementation team on a voluntary basis. Figure 6.3 (Lambourne, De Pietro, Orta-Anes, & Smith, 1992) maps out such a selection process.

It is the job of the implementation team to decide precisely how to introduce the technological change in its unit and ensure that all needed elements are in place. Any needed training, site preparation, and backup of existing data (if converting to a new software system) should be anticipated and completed before bringing the new system fully online. (Hands-on training can take place after installation but before full operation.) The implementation team must also be involved directly in the ongoing evaluation of the new system, based on the success criteria provided by the steering committee (with input from the implementation team).

Adequate staff time and resources must be allocated to enable committees to meet on a regular basis (generally biweekly) and otherwise do their work (e.g., conducting surveys during company time, etc.). Training in group process and problem identification and problem-solving skills will most likely be needed by the all three levels of committees.

Case Study: Good Health

A provider of health care insurance (which will be referred to by the pseudonym "Good Health")—sought to upgrade its dental claims processing system. Good Health employed 70 hourly and managerial employees in its claims processing department, which processed between 10,000 to 15,000 claims weekly. With its continued growth in business, Good Health's customer service had began to suffer, mainly because of its outdated manual and computer mainframe claims handling system. Employees also complained about the amount and nature of work involved in manual claims processing.

Figure 6.4 depicts the flow of dental claims through Good Health's departments. Claims first went to Receiving and Control, where they were opened, date-stamped, manually sorted, and placed the claims in inventory bins. Receiving and Control then forwarded them to Claims Processing for payment. This unit checked claims to ensure membership eligibility, that the date of service was within the benefit period, and that the amount charged was within the approved limit. Claims Processing assigned a 3-digit code to questionable claims that did not meet the needed payment

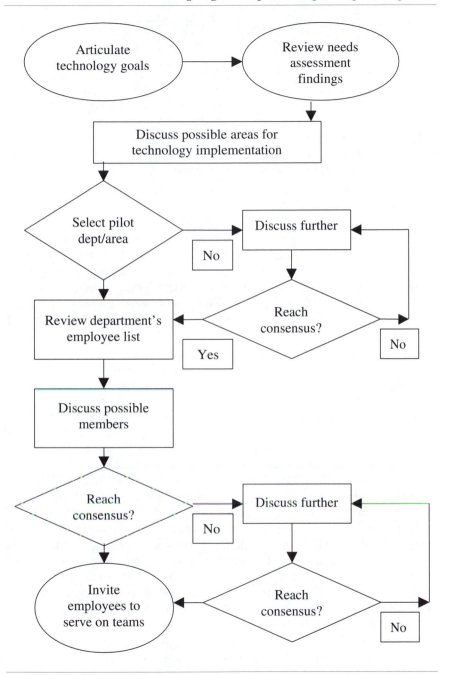

Figure 6.3   Joint Steering Committee Selection of Implementation Teams

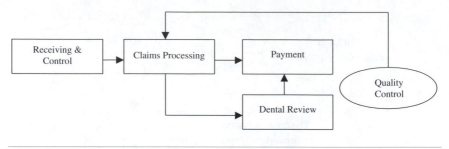

Figure 6.4   Dental Claim Processing Workflow

criteria. This unit then sent questionable claims to Dental Review, where dentists and dental hygienists determined whether and how much payment should be made for a given service. The Dental Review unit finally sent such cases to the processors for payment. The corporate Quality Control department checked the work of the claims processors for accuracy by examining work samples from each processor on a periodic basis.

High on the employee complaint list was the amount of paperwork employees were responsible for and the lack of a claims tracking system. In addition, envelopes addressed to providers were sometimes illegible or incorrect thus causing important X-rays or paperwork to be lost. The mainframe computer system used for processing the claims also lacked the capacity to allow processors to access the provider database or print labels for outgoing mail.

The departmental manager and the quality supervisor concluded that migration to a personal computer (PC) system would improve workflow, efficiency, and service to customers through greater claim accuracy and processing speed. They gave all employees in the department an opportunity to submit a "wish list" of features they wished to see in a PC system. Employees articulated three compelling needs: (a) an ability to track claims, (b) inclusion of information on a patient's dental history, and (c) general modernization of the claims processing system, including the ability to generate and print labels for outgoing mail (e.g., the return of documents and X-rays to the dental provider).

The Dental Claims department took this employee input and worked with the Information Systems (IS) department to custom develop a PC-based imaging and claims processing system. Whenever the IS team was unable to fulfill one of the "wishes," they offered an explanation and another solution. Dubbed "Newview," the newly designed system offered scanning, batching, labeling, and indexing capabilities, and used bar codes to link extraneous information and X-rays to specific cases. With a single click, the software produced a color-coded tooth chart with a narrative of the patient's claim history.

Upper management also recognized employees for their design insights. The division's senior vice president proclaimed in the company newsletter: "Every employee here deserves the credit. Your experiences and insights are what led to the design of the system." The departmental manager added: "We respect our employees' knowledge and experience. They want to do a good job, and we have been sensitive to their needs as we implemented the changes."

Because job tasks would change along with the technology, management met formally with the local union president and vice president to discuss job redesign matters. A joint steering committee oversaw changes in work redesign and training. In accordance with the collective bargaining agreement, which called for training in the face of technology-induced skill obsolescence, management provided PC training for all departmental employees. Union representatives were involved in weekly planning meetings.

In addition, the joint steering committee instituted a suggestion box system to improve bottom-up communication. Every 2 weeks during the 2-year technology planning process, a trained labor-management team reviewed the suggestions against jointly determined criteria, analyzed the issues, and, if necessary, developed a mutually agreeable action plan (involving higher labor and management leaders as necessary). The labor-management team also followed up in a timely manner with the employee(s) who had made the suggestion. Enthusiasm for the new system was enhanced by a labor-management printed circular called *Partners for Progress* that was distributed throughout the company.

Following system implementation, Good Health established a post-implementation team. This team met at first daily, then twice weekly to review system performance difficulties that were recorded daily on a log. The team consisted of supervisors, employee representatives of each unit, the IS team, and the department director. The breadth of participation and the inclusion of senior management ensured that the team had the expertise and authority needed to resolve operational problems that arose.

Labor and management both judged the new imaging and PC system to be a great improvement over the largely manual procedures it replaced. There was a noticeable decrease in the number of provider complaints, and the Quality Control department identified fewer errors. There was also a marked efficiency in claims processing, and more positive attitudes among employees about their work. One of the dentists in the Dental Review unit said that the new system made his job "100 percent easier." Similarly, a claims processor responsible for checking pricing reported in a feature article in the company newspaper that "with claim images online rather than on paper or microfilm, we can focus on improving quality and pleasing our customers."

The general consensus of all who observed and who were involved in the process was that two factors contributed to the success of the new system: (a) the involvement of end users in determining the design specifications and (b) the participation and cooperation of representatives of all major stakeholder and expert groups—users, their union representatives, supervisors and managers, and the information systems program developers—in system planning and implementation.

Lessons Learned

The University of Wisconsin Hospital and Clinics and the Good Health insurance company case studies each illustrate the benefits of participatory design—in the determination of technology specifications as well as in the implementation and postimplementation phases of change. Participatory design is not without its trials and tribulations. Mankin, Cohen, and Bikson (1997) describe the tensions that can arise when representatives from different stakeholder groups come together to design complex change. Yet they conclude, as does this author, that the benefits of user involvement in all stages of the design process far outweigh difficulties along the way. The end result of participatory design is generally the creation of systems that are relevant to user needs, boosting employee pride in the technology that they helped to bring online.

Summary

This chapter addresses two dimensions of technology design—one pertaining to the object or system design, and the other involving the manner in which implementation occurs. Social constructivism suggests that design and development of technology is influenced by social factors—culture, organizational requirements, politics, and so on. This chapter advocates participatory technology design, supported by examples from Scandinavia, Germany, the United Kingdom, and the United States.

These international examples, plus the case study from the University of Wisconsin Hospital and Clinics, illustrate the feasibility of and benefits from participatory design. The example of the clinical information system that was collaboratively designed by nurses and information systems staff, with the facilitation of a university labor studies professor, was far more appropriate to nurses' needs than the predecessor system designed without their input. This was because nurses contributed their "skilled know-how" and experience to the design process.

There are a number of prerequisites to participatory design of the technological system. One is the willingness of management to share information with the union (or employee representatives in nonunion workplaces) about business strategy and perceived technology needs. Such information sharing must take place well before the point of technology introduction. Another prerequisite is union strategy, and a third is union and employee access to technical expertise. This enables full and equal participation in the design process.

This chapter also examines the design of the technology implementation plan. An implementation process that is jointly designed and representative of the workforce will help to minimize problems during installation, start-up, and operation phases. A joint steering committee should plan and oversee the change process at the macro level of the organization; working committees and departmental implementation teams should conduct the hands-on work. A health care insurance industry case study illustrates how these teams should work together. In conclusion, the benefits of participatory design far outweigh the drawbacks.

Seven

Training and Technological Change

Effective training is a vital element of successful technological change. As seen in the Good Health case described in Chapter 6, new technology usually alters job tasks and requires that employees learn new skills. All too often in technology adoption scenarios, though, training is an afterthought that is "too little and too late." A more effective strategy is to build training into the overall technology and business strategy and offer it on the front end of the change process. Moreover, as this chapter will demonstrate, there is great value in planning and evaluating training jointly with the union (or with affected employees if there is no union present).

Training's Contribution to High-Performance Workplaces

Investment in training is as important as technology investment as a means of improving organizational performance. In a landmark 1990 study on the link between worker training and global competitiveness, the Office of Technology Assessment of the U.S. Congress (since abolished) drew the following conclusions:

- The industrial paradigm shift from mass production to flexible decentralization (shorter production runs, flexible automation, increased worker discretion) requires workers with new, higher-level skills.
- Training is linked to productivity, quality, flexibility, and effective use of technology in the best performing firms.
- Good training has a great payoff—for individuals, organizations, and the nation, whereas inadequate training is associated with downtime, defects, waste, health and safety risks, and poor customer service.
- In comparison to other industrialized countries, particularly Japan and Germany, U.S. firms do not provide enough training for their employees (1.2 to 1.8% of payroll in United States in 1988 compared to 4% in Germany).
- Federal and state governments in the United States do not provide enough support to make up for the private sector training lag (U.S. Congress, 1990).

While he was secretary of labor, Robert Reich appealed for more extensive training and education to meet the demands of changing workplaces. Using the example of automotive mechanics, he noted that in 1990, the average Ford automobile had 18% of its components controlled by computers, while a mere 4 years later, this figure had shifted to 82% (Reich, 1994).

Majchrzak (1988), among other researchers, emphasizes the link between human resource strategies and successful automation. She cites examples of poor technology performance resulting from delaying human resource planning until *after* the new technology has been installed. Among the specific training problems she mentions are (a) inadequate training budget as part of the cost-benefit calculation, (b) reliance on technology vendors for training that is not tailored to the needs of the specific workplace, and (c) use of unstructured on-the-job training (p. 155).

It is not only at the time of implementation that training is needed, but throughout the technology life cycle because skill requirements in a given workplace change as technology matures (Flynn, 1988). Case studies that Flynn conducted at 200 firms revealed that by offering training over time, some organizations could more precisely meet work and employee needs, and schedule training more flexibly than if they relied on equipment manufacturers to train employees in machine-specific skills (p. 59). However, she also noted the important role that schools and colleges can play in imparting needed skills and in assisting in workforce and economic development (pp. 149, 153).

Basic and literacy skills (reading, writing, arithmetic, and communication) are thought to be the building blocks of technology and job-specific training (Mikulecky & Kirkley, 1998). It has been estimated that on average, 20% of adults are lacking in these skill sets (U.S. Congress, 1990, p. 8;

U.S. Department of Education, 1992). Forty percent of manufacturing executives, responding to a 1991 survey by the National Association of Manufacturers, believed that worker deficiencies in basic and literacy skills inhibited their companies' ability to upgrade technology, and 37 percent saw these skill shortcomings as barriers to enhanced productivity (Bergman, 1995). These findings were corroborated by a 1993 study by the W. E. Upjohn Institute for Employment Research, which estimated that basic skills training could enhance employee productivity by 10 to 20 percent (Bergman, 1995).

Yet according to a report published by the National Alliance of Business' National Workforce Assistance Collaborative, companies seeking to "improve their bottom lines" generally focus on "adopting new technologies, reorganizing work, or providing training in technical or work process skills," arguing that "basic skills training is not a company responsibility" (Bergman, p. 2). This belief supports the practice of "investing in skilled employees who already have demonstrated their value to the firm" (Zemsky & Oedel, 1995, p. 5).

Still, employers *do* invest in training, but analyzing whether or not they provide enough training is not the central point of this chapter. Rather, this chapter's focus is on the importance of training as a component of an overall technology planning strategy. Training plan methods, and examples of successful labor-management training partnerships are also presented.

Training Program Design

If training is needed before the technology is fully operational, how do organizations go about planning a well-designed training program? First, the manager in charge of training (in large organizations this will be a separate position and in smaller ones the human resource manager generally plays this role) needs timely and accurate information about the technological changes that are anticipated—while the process is still in the planning stage. For this and other reasons, the training manager needs to be included as a member of the joint steering committee. In the example of the Brownvale plant in Chapter 1, the training manager was out of the loop when software changes were made in the automated storage and retrieval system, thus compounding the operations difficulties that ultimately occurred.

Who Will Conduct the Training?

The first question that must be addressed before designing an effective training program is whether the training will be offered "in house" or "out of house" by an external vendor (e.g., equipment vendor, training company, college or university, state extension agency, etc.). As discussed earlier in this chapter, Majchrzak (1988) and Flynn (1988) argued against equipment vendor-provided training. They are correct in advising against training that is too narrow in its focus. This advice should not be interpreted as a condemnation of all externally provided training. Many organizations lack the expertise and resources to design and deliver effective training. In that case, shopping for an appropriate training vendor may be advisable.

Training vendor selection should be based on far more than cost. An excellent example is provided by an Amcar plant (same parent company as described in Chapter 1 but different plant) in Canada. A four-person labor-management "Skilled Trades Committee on New Technology" was created as a result of the negotiated plant-level collective bargaining agreement. Because management representatives were overburdened with other duties, the two union representatives (and their alternates) essentially ran the program. They designed a comprehensive training plan for 386 trades employees. Armed with a budget of $3 million for training and administration costs, they conducted need and skill assessments, determined curricular requirements based on the results of these assessments, selected training vendors, and evaluated training effectiveness (Haddad, 1994).

The bids of training and equipment vendors were put through an elaborate process of scrutiny and were expected to be accompanied by detailed training plans. The committee established four criteria by which to analyze training plans: (a) course description, content, objectives, and outline; (b) amount of time devoted to each subject or course; (c) cost; and (d) appropriateness of the course to the trade. Once analyzed, bids were filed into color-coded binders for future reference. A management group provided most of the input on cost assessment, but the New Technology Committee could veto their recommendation and pursue the matter directly with the plant manager. Cost was not necessarily the most compelling criteria. A great deal of weight was placed on the other criteria (e.g., adequacy of time for the subject, appropriateness of the content for the trade) (Haddad, 1994).

The company benefited from the involvement of skilled union negotiators in administering the training program for trades employees. Committee members scrutinized training bids to ensure their plant was not charged for development costs for generic courses (e.g., conveyor systems) that they had already offered at other plants. In addition, a union millwright who was assisting the New Technology Committee bargained with a small machine and parts vendor to get 36,000 hours of training offered at no cost to the plant.

Steps in Training Program Design

Effective training program design is a multistep process with numerous substeps. Dick and Carey (1990) developed one of the most popular

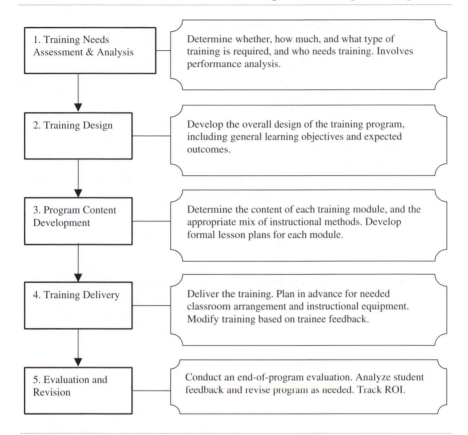

1. Training Needs Assessment & Analysis	Determine whether, how much, and what type of training is required, and who needs training. Involves performance analysis.
2. Training Design	Develop the overall design of the training program, including general learning objectives and expected outcomes.
3. Program Content Development	Determine the content of each training module, and the appropriate mix of instructional methods. Develop formal lesson plans for each module.
4. Training Delivery	Deliver the training. Plan in advance for needed classroom arrangement and instructional equipment. Modify training based on trainee feedback.
5. Evaluation and Revision	Conduct an end-of-program evaluation. Analyze student feedback and revise program as needed. Track ROI.

Figure 7.1   Steps in Training Program Design

models used by instructional designers. This model begins with identification of instructional goals, followed by instructional analysis, articulation of performance objectives, and development of test items. This author prefers the five-step Systematic Curriculum and Instructional Development (SCID) model put forth by Norton (1992) and modified and shown in Figure 7.1.

Training Needs Assessment and Analysis

Training needs assessment and analysis is the front-end part of training program design. Training needs assessment is "a process for determining goals, identifying discrepancies between goals and the status quo, and establishing priorities for action" (Burton & Merrill, 1977, pp. 21–45, cited in Benjamin, 1989). Training needs analysis involves analyzing the data from the needs assessment, and determining reasons for discrepancies

Table 7.1   Training Needs Assessment and Analysis Steps

1. Set forth strategic training objectives.	Answer these questions: Why is training needed? What is training expected to accomplish? What categories of employees need training? How does training fit into the organization's business and technology strategies?
2. Identify data needed to determine training needs and training delivery methods.	Examine job descriptions, performance appraisals (if unbiased), and all relevant existing data, including technology operation specifications from vendor. Determine what additional data are needed.
3. Decide on a method or methods for collecting this data.	Possible methods include interviews with individuals and groups of employees; observations of employees performing work; and survey questionnaires.
4. Collect the data.	Use the data collection methods determined to be most appropriate.
5. Analyze and validate the data and determine needed skill sets.	Determine patterns and trends, and cross-check written data against information gleaned from interviews and other sources.
6. Develop training needs and strategies.	Develop a prioritized statement of training needs and recommended strategies for meeting the needs.

between goals and performance through methodologies such as job analysis (Rodriguez, 1988). Training needs assessment and analysis force an organization to engage in a strategic planning process that links training goals to business and technology objectives. It also helps key players—in labor and management—determine whether their respective assessments of goals and current performance are congruent. Without a shared vision of what is needed and the route to get there, there is less chance that the training program will be successful.

Table 7.1 displays possible steps, adapted from Zemke and Rossett (1985), for conducting training needs assessment and analysis. The needed steps should be determined by a joint training committee, working in tandem with the Joint Steering Committee. Joint agreement on performance specification requirements and data collection methods builds employee trust and cooperation, and ensures that the objective is to identify areas for new learning and not employee "deficiencies."

Training Design

Once training needs have been determined, an overall design for the training program can be mapped out. This includes decisions about what general topics will be covered, the number of modules needed, whether the training will be offered during working hours, whether it will be held on consecutive days or spread across several weeks, where the training will be held, how trainees and trainers will be selected, and what equipment and materials are needed. General learning objectives should be determined for each module, and expected outcomes should be identified. Cost and staffing considerations come into play at this stage. Although training during working hours will yield the highest participation rate, this requires that replacement employees be available and in certain organizations like schools, hospitals, and law enforcement agencies it may be difficult to release even small groups of employees from their job responsibilities.

Training for technological change will generally include, at a minimum, courses in problem-solving and decision-making skills and basic computer skills (Gattiker, 1990, p. 138). Majchrzak (1988), too, advises that the curriculum in preparation for technology's arrival include generic as well as job-specific courses. To determine the right mix of relevant courses, she advocates task analysis and "early involvement of the users" in the determination of training and curricular needs (p. 181).

Program Content Development

At this stage, formal lesson plans are developed for each module. These lesson plans should include instructional objectives that specify performance outcomes (e.g., "at the end of this unit, the trainee will be able to scan a document using X software"), a list of topics (units) to be covered, readings and other material designed to clarify or expand on each unit's topic, and the identification of the instructional method to be used to cover each of the topics. Common instructional methods are lecture, discussion, exercises, on-the-job practice, and simulation. As Gattiker (1990) observes, training relying on only one instructional method "often leads to gaps in the trainee's education" (p. 139).

Training Delivery

The training is conducted according to the plan that has been developed in steps 1 to 3 in Figure 7.1. Participant reaction to each unit is observed or solicited and may be formally measured ("formative" evaluation that takes place during the training program). This information may result in changes being made while the training is in progress. For example, one common occurrence in training is that an instructor will include too much material for a given unit or module. An astute trainer will notice when trainees develop blank expressions that signify boredom, fatigue, or frustration and will do a "reality check" by asking the group to verify what they are feeling, and then adjust the content as needed. If a massive amount of material simply must be covered, the lecture should touch on the highlights and should be supplemented by a detailed, easy-to-follow training manual.

Evaluation and Revision

Evaluation involves the measurement of training effectiveness. "Summative" evaluation is conducted at the end of the program and can be developed to measure trainee reaction to and satisfaction with the training program (Level 1, the most basic and common type of evaluation), participant learning (Level 2, the extent to which measurable performance objectives have been met), changes in the learner's behavior as a result of participation in the training program (Level 3), and results (Level 4, improved organizational performance, quality, service, customer satisfaction, etc.) (Kirkpatrick, 1994).

The measurement of results can be used to assess return on investment (ROI). ROI involves comparing pre- and posttraining results on some performance measure such as productivity or customer satisfaction. To rule out the impact of independent variables other than training it is best to take pre- and posttraining measures from a control group as well as from trainees (Shelton & Alliger, 1993). ROI also involves determining the total cost (personnel, travel, course materials, facilities, and equipment) and "dollar value" of training—the latter being the difference between the value of the outcome measure before and after the training (Shelton & Alliger, 1993, p. 46). This determination requires fairly sophisticated research skills, for in addition to drawing the samples, statistical calculations must be performed to test for significant differences between the trainee and control group mean (average) scores on the performance variable(s).

Because Level 3 and 4 training is difficult and expensive to perform, some experts recommend that Level 1 (reaction) evaluation be done for all courses, Level 2 (learning) be done for those courses in which it is important for trainees to retain a body of knowledge or apply a certain skill, Level 3 (behavior) be used when the intent of the training is to change on-the-job behavior, and Level 4 (performance/results) be saved for those situations in which hard core business results are needed (Geber, 1995, p. 30).

Even the use of a simple measurement of trainee reaction using 5-point, Likert response scales (e.g., a rating system—asking participants to "rate the overall effectiveness of the instructor" with a rating scale of 5 = excellent, 4 = very good, 3 = good, 2 = fair, and 1 = poor) offers enough information on how well the training program was received to modify it before it is offered again.

Long-Range Training Strategy

Effective training depends as much on *strategy* as on having a box of training tools available and knowing how to use them. A joint (labor-management) training committee is well positioned to meet with representatives of the joint steering committee and dialogue about the strategic planning process. Training goals should flow from the strategic business and technology objectives that have been articulated by the steering committee. Many in the training community believe that "a solid understanding of the goals, processes and operations of the organization" are "core competencies" of training managers (Filipczak, 1994, p. 32). Obtaining information on product or service development strategies; industry, sector, or market trends; anticipated process changes and expected technology purchases will enable the training committee to ensure that training is developed not only to meet *current* needs, but also *projected* needs. This and a system of recurrent skill upgrading have high-performance payoffs for the business/institution and also serve as a source of employment stability for employees by ensuring that their skills remain current.

Successful Training Partnerships

Examples of three innovative and successful training partnerships were presented in Chapter 2 of this book: The Canadian Steel Trade and Employment Congress (CSTEC), the Wisconsin Regional Training Partnership (WRTP), and the Garment Industry Development Corporation (GIDC). It is useful to delve more deeply into the joint training committee operations of CSTEC and of an additional sectoral labor-management council—the Sectoral Skills Council of the Canadian Electrical and Electronics Manufacturing Industry (also known as the Sectoral Skills Council, or SSC). As these two councils (and GIDC as well) are examples of joint sectoral training councils, a definition is in order: "A joint sectoral training council is an industry-wide body of employer and trade union representatives that works to address human resource issues from a strategic and coordinated perspective" (Haddad, 1996b, p. 129).

Although the councils varied in structure, focus, and membership, each of them had programs for the training of current employees. In both cases, training programs, funded by participating companies and federal and provincial governments, offered training in generic or "portable" and industry-specific technical skills. Some also addressed basic and non-job-related training and education. Each of the councils had joint (labor-management) governing boards and training subcommittees, and two of them—CSTEC and the SSC—had active workplace-level joint training committees. At all levels of committee structure decisions were made by consensus (Haddad, 1996b).

In CSTEC, joint training committees were responsible for all aspects of training program administration. This included performance of training needs assessments (with the aid of a nationally produced guidebook), formulation of training plans that were for the most part linked to a company's overall training strategy, determination of curricula, selection of trainees, teaching of courses or hiring of instructors, evaluation of training courses, and budgeting. Committees at the workplace level also worked with education providers like community colleges to implement course transfer and equivalency agreements negotiated at the national level.

CSTEC guidelines stated that companies were to provide local training committees with information about planned technology investments during a 5-year period and other changes that might affect training needs, but some member companies were not forthcoming about future business strategy and long-term goals. Local committee members generally received paid release time to perform their duties and trainees attended training during working hours, though in "lean" periods some companies were less willing to provide these benefits (Haddad, 1995, p. 27).

In 1994, the first year that CSTEC offered training to employed workers, 14 of 35 existing joint training committees (JTCs) submitted training plans; 1 year later, the number had increased to 29 plans on behalf of 36 JTCs (Verma, Lamertz, & Warrian, 1998, p. 238). Although both salaried and hourly employees were eligible for training (Haddad, 1995), production employees composed the majority of trainees, with 54% receiving training in 1994–1995, primarily in technical skills (Verma et al., 1998, p. 239). At the national level, CSTEC developed generic courses in basic skills, steel industry general skills, and specific technical skills. These courses were "portable"—applicable from one steel mill to the next, yet directly relevant to the steel industry (Haddad, 1998).

CSTEC's development of national, industry-specific courses served to reduce development costs, which were shared across all of the companies belonging to the council. The dollar-for-dollar government matching funds lowered costs as well, as did CSTEC's negotiation of a flat per diem tuition rate with 19 colleges in six provinces (Haddad, 1998). Plant-level JTCs also worked with college faculty to develop 26 standardized courses leading to a steel industry training program (SITP) certificate, with guaranteed recognition of these courses across all 19 schools (Haddad, 1998).

The SSC of the Canadian Electrical and Electronics Manufacturing Industry was far more diverse in its industry and union membership than CSTEC. In early 1995, nearly 5 years after its founding, the SSC boasted a membership of 113 firms and seven national unions both representing more than 40,000 industry employees (Haddad, 1995; Haddad, 1998). By 1997, its membership had grown to 208 firms (Wolfe & Martin, 1998). This breadth of membership necessitated a decentralized training structure, and by 1997, 218 joint workplace training committees (JWTCs) operating at both union and nonunion firms (employee representatives served in place of union representatives at nonunion firms) had made training available to 54,500 workers at Ontario workplaces (Wolfe and Martin, 1998). JWTCs were responsible for the full range of training program administration and budget duties performed by CSTEC's plant-level committees, including planning, course selection, trainee selection, budgeting, and evaluation (Haddad, 1998).

To support the activities of the JWTCs, the SSC Board spun off three subcommittees: (a) a training subcommittee that oversaw the use of training funds and directly assisted the JWTCs; (b) an education subcommittee that worked with colleges, universities, and high schools to improve their responsiveness to the human resource needs of the electrical and electronics industries and to advocate universal recognition of courses taken from one college to the next; and (c) a joint administration committee that worked on skilled trades and apprenticeship issues. The latter subcommittee began developing commonly agreed, industry-wide skill standards, and implemented a certificate program that would enable trades employees to upgrade their skills with courses recognized throughout the industry (Haddad, 1998).

The content of plant-level training consisted of job skill upgrading, which included technical upgrading, basic skills, and interpersonal skills (62% of training fund expenditures), general (nonjob-related) training and education (20% of fund expenditures), and employee group-directed training, or "soft skills" in group process, personal improvement (communication; stress management) diversity, and political and economic issues courses (10% of fund expenditures) (Wolfe & Martin, 1998). Training was provided at community colleges (35%), on the job (31%), at external training facilities (20%), and at high schools and universities (7%) (Wolfe & Martin, 1998).

As with CSTEC's plant-level training, the SSC's plant-level training committees encountered their share of obstacles. JWTC members were released from their jobs to perform administrative and related training tasks at some firms but not at others. At plants operating "lean," if JWTC representatives and trainees were given time off the job to participate in training functions no replacement was assigned to the shop floor, thereby causing hardship and resentment among the remaining workers (Wolfe & Martin, 1998). Still, the SSC, like the CSTEC, was generally viewed as a breakthrough to the extent that labor and management were able to work together on a strategic, comprehensive industry-wide human resource development effort.

Moreover, the SSC played an important role within individual firms in protecting training budgets and encouraging them to develop greater commitment to training. One nonunion, midsize company, for example, after joining the SSC established a joint workplace training committee, hired a training director, and, with JWTC assistance, developed a strategic training plan for the entire firm, eventually assigning the JWTC control over the company's training budget totaling 3 to 4% of payroll—far more than the 1% employer training fund contribution required by SSC (Haddad, 1995, p. 64). An industry representative who sat on the national training council described the SSC's role in institutionalizing training practice and culture within firms.

> Many companies . . . don't really get serious about training. They establish budgets . . . [but] maybe if there's a business downturn or the margins are getting skinnier, the CEO will say: 'Well, let's reduce it across the board.' What we're doing here is to say that this 1% training fund cannot be touched—it is not subject to business downturns. It is dedicated for training and training alone. This is a big step forward. We are also, through the Joint Workplace Training Committees [say]ing to the companies, 'Could you please [share] your training plan for next year with us, and we will use our 1% to integrate with that plan?' That request forces a discipline that hitherto has not been in many companies, to put together a training plan and budget. I think this is one of the very significant leverages in establishing a training culture (Haddad, 1995, p. 64).

This chapter highlights these two councils not because they operated without disagreements across labor-management lines or within labor and management ranks. Nor did they fare well when the government of Ontario switched from New Democratic Party to Progressive Conservative in 1995, reducing financial and institutional support with the abolition of the Ontario Training and Adjustment Board (Bradford, 1998). What these councils illustrate is the value in strategic and cooperative approaches to training and skills upgrading. Moreover, training programs at each of the councils benefited from the involvement of plant-level labor-management representatives involved in all facets of onsite planning and administration. This ensured greater participation of trainees and greater relevance of course offerings to plant and employee needs.

Organizations adopting new technology cannot afford to leave training to chance or convenience, or to neglect it altogether. Once after this author was interviewed about technology issues by the host of a university television program, the program technicians pointed to a closet that was packed full of computer-controlled equipment that they said their director had purchased but never taught them how to use. There it sat, collecting dust. Although most organizations do not relegate their technology purchases to the closet, they nonetheless fail to fully reap the maximum performance benefits because training is not a facet of their overall technology and business strategies.

Creating a Learning Organization

It is not only training that makes for successful technology adoption and improved performance, but the extent to which the organization fosters a climate of continual learning. Since the appearance of Peter Senge's 1990 book *The Fifth Discipline*, the concept of organizational learning has become fashionable in management circles. Building on the earlier work of Chris Argyris and Donald Schon (1978), Senge defines a learning organization as "a group of people working together to collectively enhance their capacities to create results that they truly care about" (Fuller & Keys, 1998). He views organizations as complex, organic systems or "organisms," with teams as the core performance unit and with distributed leadership, even among nonmanagers (Zemke, 1999, p. 40).

Definitions of this concept abound. Garvin (1993, as cited in King, 2001) defines a learning organization as "an organization skilled at creating, acquiring, and transferring knowledge, and at modifying its behavior to reflect new knowledge and insights (p. 12). Sitkin, Sutcliffe, and Weick (1999) state that organizational learning is "a change in an organization's response repertoire" (e.g., skills, routines, capabilities). Argyris draws a distinction between "single loop" or routine learning and "double loop" learning—that which challenges the status quo through reflective action (Abernathy, 1999, p. 80).

The concept of reflective action has its roots in the writings of earlier generations of educational theorists. Active involvement of the learner, facilitated by a learner-centered curricula and teaching methods, was promoted by the progressive philosopher John Dewey nearly a century ago and in the 1970s by the activist Brazilian educator Paulo Freire, among others. Both of these thinkers saw the empowering potential of education not only for individuals but for democratic societal values.

Those who have recently embraced the learning organization fad appear to be largely unaware that a subset of adult education theorists in the United States and abroad has long argued that the workplace should be a theater of continual learning that compliments and advances formal education and training. Adult educators recognize that "learning can result from virtually any adult experience" (Verner, 1963, p. 232). The workplace can serve theoretically as a learning laboratory, with "human participants . . . at the center of the creation of knowledge and meaningful activity" (Pipan, 1989, p. 169). In the context of the workplace, "reflective action" is defined by Kornbluh and Greene (1989) as "time devoted to discussion for work planning and problem solving . . . [that is] integrate[d] into work schedules" (p. 268).

Yet as Pipan (1989) observes, the manner in which the workplace is structured can either facilitate or inhibit learning. Kornbluh & Greene (1989) echo this view, in their assertion that the "work situation presents the opportunity for a powerful learning mechanism through structuring the work in groups that assume responsibility for decisions about the work they perform and how they perform it" (p. 263). In short, the work environment "must stimulate workers to feel the need to learn more" through varied activities that build on preexisting knowledge and skill, job autonomy and discretion, performance feedback mechanisms, and social or cognitive rewards for performance (Leymann, 1989, p. 133). Beyond self-directed work groups and job structure, Pelz (1976, cited in Leymann, 1989) adds that creative problem solving at work requires access to organizational resources and economic security. Employees must be assured that by applying their knowledge and creativity to the job, they will not face displacement through the transfer of that knowledge to a computer program or to lesser-paid coworkers.

An appreciation for the adult education and workplace learning concepts just described is essential to the design of effective training programs. This point is emphasized by Hirschhorn, Gilmore, and Newell (1989), who assert that "because trainers focus on skills rather than on situations, ignore roles and relationships, and separate the training encounter from the natural world of work they cannot help people learn the roles they need to work effectively in a post-industrial economy" (pp. 188–189).

The solution, according to these authors, is for trainers to view themselves and to be viewed by managers as "consultants to the learning process" and "designers of learning encounters" (p. 198) in which students learn deductively and from one another, not merely from the expertise of the trainer. This can be a difficult role for trainers to play given the expectation from the managers who hire them and the trainees themselves that they deliver clever lectures, embellished with "war stories," and that they have ready answers to every problem brought forth by classroom participants.

Effective training must also "bridge the natural world of work and the artificial world of training" (Hirschhorn et al., 1989, p. 199). Simulation is a training technique that can help to link these two theaters of learning. Hirschhorn, through his exhaustive research on what factors led to the near disaster at the Three Mile Island (TMI) nuclear power plant in Pennsylvania in 1979, offers compelling evidence to support his assertion that training and work practice need to be integrated. Inappropriate design of controls by TMI engineers, who were set apart from daily operations on the shop floor, was one variable that contributed to operator misinterpretation of warning signals. Unanticipated contingencies that were not planned for was another factor (Hirschhorn, 1984).

But the leading cause of operator error was the design of training, which "separate[d] learning from work" (Hirschhorn, 1984, p. 114). In TMI training exercises involving abnormal operations, emergency equipment and instrumentation performed correctly. Instead, training exercises should also have been conducted under crisis conditions with faulty emergency equipment (p. 89). Moreover, operators were taught cause-and-effect reasoning in rote, simplistic fashion, with some introductory theory and "single-fault" response requirements. Hirschhorn detected that "synthetic reasoning" was needed, a cyclical rather than linear process, in which "the range of possible causes is narrowed as more information is received" (p. 90), thereby guiding them from symptoms to causes (p. 91).

The proposed remedy is threefold. One required element is deeper theoretical information that conveys "breadth of operation" with "depth of understanding" (p. 94) so that workers comprehend how an operation works in its entirety and the interrelatedness of subsystems. Another is training simulation that presents unanticipated circumstances/system failures in ways that require the broader analytical reasoning described above. A third is the broadening of job tasks to incorporate more knowledge-based, skilled work. Guided by the principles of sociotechnical integration, workplaces can use self-directed work teams and job rotation as vehicles for continuous learning and thinking on the job (Hirschhorn, 1984, pp. 115–116).

The need for continuous learning brings this chapter's discussion of "learning organizations" full circle. If there remains any question about the need for continuous learning within organizations, Fulmer, Gibbs, and Keys (1998) proclaim that "organizational learning may be the source of the only sustainable competitive advantage" (p. 6), while keeping in mind that "organizational learning is a long-term activity that will build competitive advantage over time and requires sustained management attention, commitment, and effort" (Goh, 1998, p. 15). Reading Senge's book or attending a management seminar on learning organizations is merely the first step in a long-term change process.

Summary

New technology nearly always changes job tasks and skill requirements; therefore, employee training must be a component of the overall technology planning strategy. Studies conclude that training is linked to competitiveness and to successful automation and is needed not only at the point of equipment or software implementation but throughout the technology life cycle. Effective training program design requires an appreciation for adult education principles, and a recognition that training must simulate the natural world of work. Research on the disaster at Three Mile Island points to poorly constructed training as a leading cause of operator error, for training at the nuclear facility emphasized rote cause-and-effect reasoning instead of an analytical process that guided them from symptoms to causes.

When designing a training program, consideration must first be given to the question of whether the training will be conducted internally or externally. If outside trainers are to be used, their training plan should be analyzed for content and applicability, not merely cost. A five-step process is suggested for designing an effective training program: (a) training needs assessment and analysis, (b) overall program design, (c) program content development, (d) training delivery methodology, and (e) evaluation and revision. A long-range training strategy will help to ensure that training is planned not only for current needs, but also for projected needs.

The CSTEC and the SSC serve as examples of successful training partnerships. Both have strategic-level bipartite governing committees and plant-level joint committees that plan and oversee workplace-based training. At the national level, they have been successful in developing skill standards and portability agreements and have worked with community colleges to develop a standardized certificate program constructed of nationally recognized courses. The payoff at the plant level has been equally impressive, with the joint training committees adding value to training dollars allocated by the companies.

In addition to having a sound training plan, the workplace should be structured in such a way so as to foster a climate of organizational learning, by stimulating curiosity and encouraging analytical thinking and problem solving in a context of job security. In summary, training must not be an afterthought, but rather a strategic facet of the technology planning process.

Eight

Evaluating and Managing Change for Optimal Performance

Evaluation is the last stage in the technology adoption life cycle (see Figure 3.1 in Chapter 3). The purpose of evaluation is to ensure that the technology is meeting organizational, business, and performance objectives. Because the technology adoption life cycle is a circular process rather than a linear one, evaluation is not really the "last" stage in the process because information collected enables ongoing management and feeds back into business strategy.

Conducting the Technology Evaluation

Basic Evaluation Questions

Evaluation must be guided by the strategic technology goals established before the purchase and installation of the new equipment or system(s). Table 4.1 (in Chapter 4) presented some common goals for introducing new technology. Table 8.1 elaborates on those goals, adding fundamental

Table 8.1   Basic Areas for Evaluation

Technology Goal	Evaluation Questions
Efficiency	• Has the new technology improved our rate of output? • Has the new technology improved product/service delivery time?
Cost	• Has the new technology led to cost savings beyond efficiency, as in reduced scrap or wasted time? Do these benefits outweigh the cost of the technology?
Product/Service Quality	• Has the new technology led to greater consistency of product/service/higher student test scores? • Has it resulted in fewer customer complaints? • Has it improved our reputation in the marketplace?
Flexibility	• Has the new technology enabled us to customize our products/services? • Has it improved our ability to meet variations in demand?
Health and Safety	• Has the new technology enabled us to lower our accident and injury rates? • Has it led to fewer sick days? • Has it improved workstation comfort?
Quality of Working Life	• Have job skill requirements increased as a result of the new technology? • Has employee job satisfaction risen since the new technology was introduced? • Has the new technology led to lower absenteeism and higher employee retention? • Have new jobs been created because of new demand for products or services made possible by the new technology?
Market Share	• Has the new technology created market opportunities through the development of new products or services?
Communication	• Has the new technology led to improved intra-organizational communication? • Has it led to improved communication with customers, suppliers, and other external constituencies?
Labor Relations	• Has the new technology affected the labor-management relationship?
Rewards	• Has the new technology resulted in greater profit-sharing or gain-sharing bonuses? • Has it provided job and career upgrading opportunities?

evaluation questions. Evaluating technology's impact on the organization is as important as measuring its impact on business performance.

Evaluation Measures and Methods

The type of evaluation most applicable to measuring the effect of new technology on performance and other outcomes is called an "impact assessment" (Rossi & Freeman, 1993, p. 36). This evaluation involves defining objectives and success criteria. The goals and evaluation questions in Table 8.1 are useful starting points. Adding specific ways to measure success completes the picture. For example, it may be determined that a 10% reduction in employee absenteeism would be a good measure of improved quality of working life.

Technology effectiveness measures require definition of broad, ambiguous goals. For example, technology may be expected to improve firm performance, yet "performance" may refer to actual production or service output, the process leading to such output, organizational functioning, impact on customers, or business and financial results. Measurement depends on the goals that the new technology is expected to meet, and on the industry sector in which the organization is operating. Take for example, a manufacturing firm that establishes a goal of improved efficiency for its new technology. One measure of efficiency is "unit labor hours"—the dollar value and number of labor hours needed to produce one unit of output.

Such a measurement would not easily apply to nonmanufacturing sectors such as education or health care. In an educational organization, a measure of efficiency might be the number of hours spent calculating student grades and progress. Presumably a software program that automatically calculates grades and tracks student progress would allow teachers to spend more time preparing for class or interacting with students in between class periods. In contrast, an efficiency measure might be altogether inappropriate to the health care sector. It has been argued that cost, effectiveness, and safety are the most important criteria for the evaluation of new medical devices, procedures, and drugs (Benda, 1999).

Once an organization lists and defines its objectives, the next step in any evaluation is to construct the research design. In order to determine whether the outcome (e.g., a 10% reduction in employee absenteeism) is the result of the new technology and not some other factor, one of the most rigorous and accepted research designs is a pretest-posttest with randomized control and experimental groups. The experimental group in this case would be those who are working with the new technology and the control would be a comparable group of employees who are not working with the new technology being evaluated. Random assignment means that a sample of the workforce would be assigned in a random manner either to the experimental or control groups (Fitz-Gibbon & Morris, 1987; Rossi & Freeman, 1993).

Practically speaking, it is difficult to construct and test a control group when implementing new technology. It may be the case that the technology is introduced throughout the workplace, or that nonusers have different characteristics than users of technology. An alternative evaluation method is the single group time-series design, in which measures of outcome variables (e.g., efficiency, customer service) are taken from the experimental group only (technology users) before the intervention (the new technology introduction) and again repeatedly at regular time intervals (such as monthly or quarterly (Fitz-Gibbon & Morris, 1987). This is a bit more feasible to implement, and although it is not possible to link changes over time solely to the technology, longitudinal measurement paints a useful picture of long-term technology performance.

Because of the "learning curve" associated with new technology, performance generally declines for a few weeks or even months after installation. It takes time for the system and those programming, using, and maintaining it to operate flawlessly, for the "bugs" to be worked out of the software, and for purchased hardware and software to be fine-tuned and customized to local needs. Postimplementation time series measures should therefore be delayed at least one month after technology installation.

Technology Evaluation in Practice

The Needmore Elementary School in rural Bedford, Indiana, sought in 1998 to assess whether technology used for individualized instruction improved teaching, learning, productivity, and communication (Branzburg, 2001). The school district followed a procedure advocated in this book—using a broad-based group of stakeholders to define benchmarks against which progress could be measured. Stakeholders in this case included teachers, community members, administrators, and school board members. Recognizing the value that professional researchers could apply to the process, the district engaged the services of Indiana University. A software program called GroupSystems was applied to the benchmark identification, criteria ranking, and selection process (Branzburg, 2001).

This led to the construction of an evaluation questionnaire that measured (on a 5-point Likert scale), among other factors, the extent to which teachers felt students had attained a benchmark learning goal. Teachers also rated themselves on the integration of technology into their lesson plans. Qualitative research methods were also used, including interviews with teachers and administrators, classroom observation, and review of student portfolios and state test scores. After determining which benchmarks had been attained, and assuring teachers that lower scores would not be linked to job performance, the school pledged to engage in the self-study evaluation process on a continuing, regular basis. This was done to provide an ongoing picture of student performance and professional development (Branzburg, 2001).

The importance of involving technology users in the determination of evaluation criteria is recognized beyond the field of K-12 education. Those who write about the health care industry note that "technology cannot be assessed in a vacuum" and therefore the input of clinician practitioners with recent experience in health care delivery related to the technology is essential to effective evaluation (Benda, 1999, p. 22).

A final and cautionary note about technology evaluation is in order. First, outcomes will be different at various stages of the implementation process, hence the need to take multiple measures as suggested earlier in this chapter. Second, the evaluation design should attempt to isolate the effects of technology from other factors. Accomplishing such a separation is difficult, but a research design that identifies performance benchmarks is one way of attempting it (McNabb, Hawkes, & Rouk, 1999), especially if repeated measures are taken as recommended earlier in this chapter. Technology, therefore, becomes a tool for realizing these benchmark goals, and not an end unto itself.

Ongoing Technology Management

Evaluation is the last step in the technology adoption life cycle, but completion of evaluation does not signal an end to the process of technological change. Successful technology use requires ongoing management, learning, and fine-tuning.

Ongoing management refers to a multitude of tasks designed to ensure that the technology functions in an optimal manner. These tasks appear in the box below. The implementation teams described in Chapter 6 play a central role, along with departmental management, in the performance of these maintenance tasks. Feedback data that is regularly and, in some cases, automatically available as a feature of the technology should be reviewed and analyzed. This includes information on all relevant dimensions of performance as well as on breakdowns. In addition, a formal evaluation of the type described earlier in this chapter should be performed at scheduled intervals.

Box 8.1   ONGOING TECHNOLOGY MANAGEMENT TASKS

- ◆ Analysis of feedback data
- ◆ Periodic evaluation
- ◆ Information sharing
- ◆ Scheduled maintenance
- ◆ Regular training

A third important feature of an ongoing management program is the sharing of information pertaining to technology performance with other departments and units or schools in the case of K-12 education. This sharing enables dissemination of best practice and minimizes problems as other units adopt similar technologies. Representatives of implementation teams from different departments should meet periodically to discuss optimal and poor technology performance and measures that have been taken to remedy problems.

Scheduling maintenance on a regular basis is an essential component of a technology management program, for it prevents the untimely breakdown and malfunction of equipment. Although this advice is common sense, surprisingly few organizations schedule regular maintenance because of an unwillingness to interrupt operations to perform it. This approach, although understandable, is shortsighted for as the adage goes, "an ounce of prevention is worth a pound of cure."

The establishment of regular training in an environment that promotes continuous learning is another essential feature of ongoing technology management. "Refresher" courses or those that go beyond basic knowledge of the software or hardware to teach more advanced functions can help to maximize employee and technology performance. Employees using the technology and members of the implementation team might also serve as trainers of employees in other departments or units that plan to adopt the same or a similar technology. This train-the-trainer approach has a knowledge spillover effect, and peer training is particularly effective in reducing employee anxiety.

In short, ongoing technology management ensures that it is the organization that guides technology use, rather than the other way around. Continuous technology management also serves to increase the positive performance aspects of technology and minimize system failure.

Institutionalizing a Strategic Partnership Approach to Change

Perhaps the most neglected aspect of change is the effort needed to sustain it. Similar to a dieter who loses weight and then promptly regains it, organizations sometimes make dramatic and positive transformations, only to revert back to the old ways once short-term goals are met. This was certainly the case at the Amcar plant that produced the Flash automobile as described in Chapter 1. That plant made extraordinary changes in structure, culture, and labor relations, resulting in an impressive reduction in product lead time, among other benefits.

Yet following the successful launch of the new product, Amcar did not follow through. The plant manager who encouraged union-represented employee involvement in product design and assembly decisions—becoming popular on the shop floor in the process—was transferred to another plant to oversee another new product launch. Local union leaders perceived that the new manager, who was far less popular on the shop floor, lacked enthusiasm for joint union-management programs that had thrived under the leadership of his predecessor. More than 200 grievances were filed during one of his early years as plant manager, and "conditions per 100 vehicles"—an automotive measure of poor product quality—also rose (Haddad, 2000a).

This story is all too common. It points to the short-term focus and unilateral design of certain innovations, and to the lack of attention paid to watering and growing organizational change once it has sprouted. During the 1960s and 1970s, many organizations adopted "Quality of Worklife" programs—often in response to wildcat strikes or other extreme manifestations of job boredom and worker alienation. Although some of these programs were considered "successful" and others "failures," most were relatively short-lived. The faddish nature of new managerial initiatives is cynically referred to by frontline employees as the "flavor of the month" as stated earlier in this volume.

The reason for such pessimism is that notwithstanding some examples to the contrary (Bluestone & Bluestone, 1992), many employee involvement programs have been neither strategic nor participative. Conceived by upper management and fostered in a top-down manner, most such programs are limited in scope and influence, and subject to the vagaries of the business climate. Worker input is solicited regarding where to place vending machines in an employee break area, but not on crucial technology, product, process, or business decisions. Some employers have even tried to use involvement committees to bypass union structures and collective bargaining (Nissen, 1997; Sagie & Koslowsky, 2000, p. 5), causing unions to discourage their members from participating, or take a hands-off approach, providing little if any guidance on the parameters of participation. In some instances where the cooperative relationship between company and union was working smoothly, the plug was pulled and plants even closed when demand for products or services declined (this was the fate of General Motors' Fiero plant, despite its cooperative labor relations).

How, then, can change be sustained? Structurally, a permanent joint steering committee (see Chapter 6 for structure and function of these committees) can provide the leadership needed to ensure continuation of the innovations made. The steering committee must be vested with *authority*, not merely responsibility, and involved in *designing* the change process, not merely in implementing it. Decision making must be bilateral, not merely participative with management retaining all control. A formal process must be established for ongoing use of employee suggestions in technology design or selection and implementation plans. In a unionized workplace, the participative process should be embedded in the collective bargaining agreement to give it legitimacy, establish that it is truly "joint" and ensure that it is not "here today and gone tomorrow."

Box 8.2   INGREDIENTS FOR SUSTAINING A STRATEGIC
PARTNERSHIP APPROACH TO CHANGE

- ♦ Joint steering committee
- ♦ Committee structure and authority embedded in collective bargaining agreement
- ♦ Adequate resources
- ♦ Leadership
- ♦ Internal information sharing
- ♦ Commitment
- ♦ Training
- ♦ Equitable rewards

Another ingredient for sustained change is the commitment of adequate resources to the change process. Committees and teams must have access to information and data needed to inform the decision-making process and may require the assistance of internal or external technical personnel who can aggregate statistical information and analyze trends. Consultants may be needed to provide training and support in collaborative decision making. Funding will be required to finance the cost of training, time spent at committee meetings and training, and internal and external publicity about joint activities and accomplishments.

Leadership and commitment are two crucial components of innovation longevity. As discussed in Chapter 5, "leadership" means having a strategic vision that looks toward a future of new possibilities. This vision must be informed by broad-based input and articulated in ways that all in the organization can hear. Leadership means valuing employees for their knowledge and input and listening to and acting on their concerns and ideas. Employees, along with external customers and members of the public, can suggest ways of improving services, products, working life, and opportunities for individual and collective growth. Leadership also means treating the union as a partner in strategic decisions—at the point of design and conception, not merely at the implementation stage. Effective leaders are able to make courageous decisions and to inspire employees to make the leap beyond what is known and comfortable.

Commitment is another critical ingredient for sustaining innovative change. Commitment means that the strategic partners must not bail out of the change process when it becomes difficult, or when their constituents criticize their collaborative involvement. Strategic partners must work through difficult issues to arrive at consensus and defend their decisions through education of their respective constituencies. Information must be shared internally, so that the leadership is better able to maintain the fine balance of leading while not moving too far ahead of the membership. Union and public sector leaders who fail to communicate with their members or the general public will be promptly voted out of office.

Participation must become embedded in an organization's structure and long-term practice and must even be a measure of good performance in management reward and compensation systems. However, if managers feel coerced, they may work to subvert joint processes. Employees, whether managers or those on the frontline of operations, must not be made to fear retaliation or retribution for what they reveal honestly in meetings.

Finally, a system for equitably sharing the gains of improved performance must be established. This sharing may take any number of forms, such as financial rewards (e.g., gain-sharing bonuses), or job security resulting from a more competitive company, or increased investment in training and education. All eight of the factors listed in Box 8.2 work in tandem to enrich and sustain the process of collaborative and strategic change.

The Strategic Partnership Payoff

Some will conclude that the strategic partnership approach to technological change advocated in this volume is too time consuming and costly to be practical. My argument in reply is that forging ahead and installing new technology *without* strategy and partnership is far more costly and ultimately more time consuming. The Learning Elementary school, Community Police, and Brownvale plant cases in Chapter 1 illustrate this point. These scenarios of ineffective technology adoption are all too common in workplaces in a variety of industries.

If there is peril in top-down decision making, is there payoff in partnership approaches to technological and general management practice? The cases presented in this volume strongly point to that conclusion. A growing body of research also supports that same position. In a survey of large manufacturing companies, William Cooke, director of the Douglas A. Fraser Center for Workplace Issues, found that among unionized firms, those with jointly (union and management) administered employee participation attained significantly greater product quality than did those with adversarial labor-management relationships and no participation programs (Cooke, 1992).

In another study based on survey data from more than 100 unionized manufacturing firms, Cooke (1989, 1990) found that the firms with the highest productivity and quality were those in which union leaders were strongly and actively involved in labor-management steering committees. He further concluded that joint activities were less effective in plants with declining employment levels than in those with stable or increasing employment.

In conclusion, the evidence presented throughout this book suggests that organizations are missing opportunities for high performance and technology success if they fail to engage employees and their designated union representatives in strategic technology planning, design, and decision making.

Reviewing the Steps of a Strategic Partnership Approach to Technology Management

Figure 8.1 reviews the steps involved in establishing and maintaining a strategic partnership approach to technology management. The first step, before making technology decisions, is for management and the union (or employee representative in a nonunion workplace) to commit to work in a collaborative partnership fashion.

Business strategy formulation then precedes determination of technology strategy, which in turn leads to and is influenced by a technology needs assessment. Once a decision is made to adopt new technology, the technology planning process ensues in joint collaborative fashion. Technology planning includes cost-benefit analysis, assessment of the

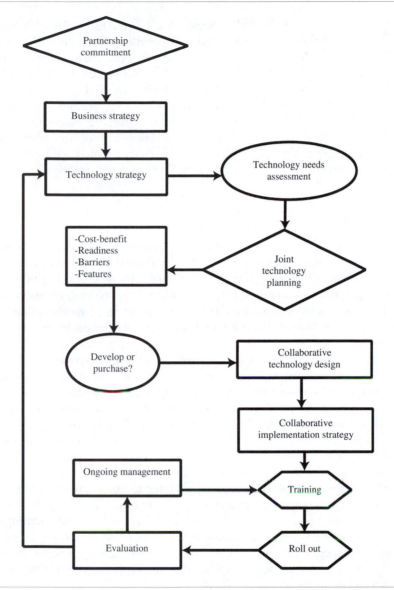

Figure 8.1   A Strategic Partnership Approach to Technology Management

readiness for technological change, identification of potential barriers and ways of overcoming them, and decisions about the required features of the new technology.

The next step is deciding whether to develop the technology "inhouse" or purchase it from an external vendor. Regardless of which option is chosen, design specifications are needed and collaboratively mapped out. A jointly determined implementation strategy follows, using the multilevel team structure outlined in Chapter 6. Training is a vital component of the implementation strategy, and precedes technology rollout. In addition, training may occur after rollout as part of the ongoing management process. Evaluation of the technology's effectiveness also occurs after rollout, and the information gleaned from this process feeds into ongoing management. Evaluation data also informs future technology strategy.

Summary

Evaluation is needed to ensure that new technology has met its intended objectives. Among the issues typically measured in evaluation are whether or not the new technology improved efficiency, cost, quality, flexibility, health and safety, quality of working life, communication, labor relations, market share, and rewards. There are various methodologies for conducting performance evaluation, and the challenge in any research design is to isolate technology effects from other variables. The best strategy is to conduct multiple measures of performance over time.

Successful technological change does not end with evaluation. Ongoing management of the change process is also needed. This includes analysis of feedback data, periodic evaluation, information sharing, scheduled maintenance, and regular training. To achieve long-term success, organizations must institutionalize a strategic partnership approach to change that is embedded in managerial structure and practice.

This chapter ends with a summary model reviewing the steps involved in a strategic partnership approach to technology management. It is argued that this approach to managing technological change is one that organizations cannot afford to bypass. Evidence presented throughout this book suggests that organizations miss opportunities for high performance and technology success if they fail to engage employees and their designated union representatives in strategic technology planning, design, and decision making.

References

Abernathy, D. J. (1999). A chat with Chris Argyris. *Training and Development,* 53(5), 80–84.

Adler, P. S. (1993). Time-and-motion regained. *Harvard Business Review, 71*(1), 97–108.

Alvin, C., Roberts, S., Schultz, F., Trimborn, S., & Emspak, F. (1998, April). *Planning and designing new technology together.* Workshop presentation at the Federal Mediation and Conciliation Service's Ninth National Labor-Management Conference, Chicago.

Argryis, C., & Schon, D. (1978). *Organizational learning: A theory of action perspective.* Reading, MA: Addison-Wesley.

Badawy, M. K. (1988). Technology management education: Alternative models. *California Management Review, 4*(4), 94–116.

Badham, R. (1995). Managing sociotechnical change: A configuration approach to technology implementation. In J. Benders, J. de Haan, & D. Bennett (Eds.), *The symbiosis of work and technology* (pp. 77–95). London: Taylor & Francis.

Banbury, C. (1999). Life cycle. In R. C. Dorf (Ed.), *The technology management handbook* (pp. 14-25–14-38). Boca Raton, FL: CRC Press.

Bancroft, N. H. (1992). *New partnerships for managing technological change.* New York: John Wiley.

Banke, P., Brödner, P., González, J., & Oehike, P. (1997). *Technology design and work organization.* Unpublished paper. European Work and Technology Consortium. Northrhine-Westphalia, Germany: Institute for Work and Technology.

Benda, C. G. (1999). Evaluating technology is a painstaking journey. *Managed Healthcare, 9*(1), 22.

Benders, J., de Haan, J., & Bennett, D. (1995). Symbiotic approaches: Contents and issues. In J. Benders, J. de Haan, & D. Bennett (Eds.), *The symbiosis of work and technology* (pp. 1–11). London: Taylor & Francis.

Benjamin, S. (1989). A closer look at needs analysis and needs assessment: Whatever happened to the systems approach? *Performance and Instruction, 28*(9), 12–16.

Benner, P. (2000). Learning through experience and expression: Skillful ethical comportment in nursing practice. In D. C. Thomasma & J. L. Kissell (Eds.), *The health care professional as friend and healer: Building on the work of Edmund D. Pellegrino* (pp. 49–64). Washington, DC: Georgetown University Press.

Benner, P. (2001). Taking a stand on experiential learning and good practice. *American Journal of Critical Care, 10*(1), 60–62.

Berggren, C. (1992). *Alternatives to lean production: Work organization in the Swedish auto industry.* Ithaca, NY: ILR Press.

Bergman, T. (1995). Basic workplace skills: The foundation for productivity improvement. *Workforce Briefs: National Workforce Assistance Collaborative.* Annapolis Junction, MD: National Alliance of Business.

Berth, R. (1997). *Wisconsin Regional Training Partnership.* Presentation at the NIST-MEP Workforce Working Group Meeting, Milwaukee, Wisconsin. Information updated via telephone interview, August 26, 1998.

Blackburn, P., Coombs, R., & Green, K. (1985). *Technology, economic growth and the labour process.* London: Macmillan.

Blauner, R. (1964). *Alienation and freedom: The factory worker and his industry.* Chicago: University of Chicago Press.

Bluestone, B., & Bluestone, I. (1992). *Negotiating the future: A labor perspective on American business.* New York: Basic Books.

Blumberg, P. (1968). *Industrial democracy: The sociology of participation.* London: Constable.

Bradford, N. (1998). Ontario's experiment with sectoral initiatives: Labour market and industrial policy, 1985–1996. In M. Gunderson & A. Sharpe (Eds.), *Forging business-labour partnerships: The emergence of sector councils in Canada* (pp. 158–189). Toronto: University of Toronto Press.

Branzburg, J. (2001). How well is it working? *Technology & Learning, 21*(7), 24–35.

Braun, E. (1998). *Technology in context: Technology assessment for managers.* Englewood Cliffs, NJ: Prentice Hall.

Bright, J. R. (1958). *Automation and management.* Boston: Harvard University Graduate School, Division of Research.

Brodner, P. (1996). Participation: A strategy for Europe's industrial renewal. In M. Gold (Ed.), *European participation monitor.* Dublin, Ireland: European Foundation for the Improvement of Living and Working Conditions.

Brown, S. L., & Eisenhardt, K. M. (1998). *Competing on the edge: Strategy as structured chaos.* Boston: Harvard Business School Press.

Butera, F., & Thurman, J. E. (1984). *Automation and work design: A study prepared by the International Labour Office.* Amsterdam, Netherlands: North-Holland.

Cammann, C., Fichman, M., Jenkins, G. D., & Klesh, J. R. (1983). Assessing the attitudes and perceptions of organizational members. In S. E. Seashore, E. E. Lawler, P. H. Mirvis, & C. Cammann (Eds.), *Assessing organizational change: A guide to methods, measures, and practices* (pp. 71–138). New York: John Wiley.

Cardullo, M. W. (1999). Technology life cycles. In R. C. Dorf (Ed.), *The technology management handbook* (2-44–3-49). Boca Raton, FL: CRC Press.

Cleland, D. I., & Bursic, K. M. (1992). *Strategic technology management: Systems for products and processes.* New York: AMACOM.

Chaykowski, R. P. (1998). The role of sector initiatives in the Canadian industrial relations system. In M. Gunderson & A. Sharpe (Eds.), *Forging business-labour partnerships: The emergence of sector councils in Canada* (pp. 295–315). Toronto: University of Toronto Press.

Cohen-Rosenthal, E. (1997). Sociotechnical systems and unions: Nicety or necessity. *Human Relations, 50*(5), 585–604.

Cooke, W. N. (1989). Improving productivity and quality through collaboration. *Industrial Relations, 28*(2), 299–319.

Cooke, W. N. (1990). *Labor-management cooperation: New partnerships or going in circles?* Kalamazoo, MI: Upjohn Institute for Employment Research.

Cooke, W. N. (1992). Product quality improvement through employee participation: The effects of unionization and joint union-management administration. *Industrial and Labor Relations Review, 46*(1), 119–134.

Cooke, W. N. (1994). Employee participation programs, groups-based incentives, and company performance: A union non-union comparison. *Industrial and Labor Relations Review, 47*(4), 594–609.

Corbett, J. M. (1990). Design for human-machine interfaces. In M. Warner, W. Wobbe, & P. Brödner (Eds.), *New technology and manufacturing management: Strategic choices for flexible production systems* (pp. 113–124). Chichester, UK: John Wiley.

Dick, W., & Carey, L. (1990). *The systematic design of instruction.* New York: HarperCollins.

Dunphy, D. (1996). Organizational change in corporate settings. *Human Relations, 49*(5), 541–547.

Early, S., & Witt, M. (1982). How European unions cope with new technology. *Monthly Labor Review, 105*(9), 37–38.

Elden, M., Havn, V., Levin, M., Nilssen, T., Rasmussen, B., & Veium, K. (1982). *Good technology is not enough: Automation and work design in Norway.* Trondheim, Norway: Institute for Social Research in Industry.

Fletcher, G. (1998). A historical perspective on sector councils. In M. Gunderson & A. Sharpe (Eds.), *Forging business-labour partnerships: The emergence of sector councils in Canada.* Toronto: University of Toronto Press.

Flynn, P. M. (1988). *Facilitating technological change: The human resource challenge.* Cambridge, MA: Ballinger.

Filipczak, B. (1994). The training manager in the '90s. *Training, 31*(6), 31–35.

Finzel, B. D., & Abraham, S. E. (1996). Bargaining over new technology: Possible effects of removing legal constraints. *Journal of Economic Issues, 30*(3), 777–795.

Fitz-Gibbon, C. T., & Morris, L. L. (1987). *How to design a program evaluation.* Newbury Park, CA: Sage.

Ford, D., & Ryan, C. (1981). Taking technology to market. *Harvard Business Review, 59*(2), 117–126.

Fuller, R. M., & Keys, J. (1998). A conversation with Peter Senge: New developments in organizational learning. *Organizational Dynamics, 27*(2), 33–42.

Fulmer, R. B., Gibbs, P., & Keys, J. B. (1998). The second generation learning organizations: New tools for sustaining competitive advantage. *Organizational Dynamics, 27*(2), 6–20.

Garment Industry Development Corporation. (1998). *GIDC News, 8*(3), 2.

Garment Industry Development Corporation. (1995). Mayor Guiliani joins fashion industry in celebrating 10th anniversary of Garment Industry Development Corporation. *GIDC News, 5*(1), 1.

Gash, D. C. (1987). The use of microcomputers as political tools. *Industrial Relations Research Association: Proceedings of the fortieth annual meeting*. Madison, WI: Industrial Relations Research Association.

Gattiker, U. E. (1990). *Technology management in organizations*. Newbury Park, CA: Sage.

Gattiker, U. E., & Ulhoi, J. P. (1999). The matrix organization revisited. In R. C. Dorf (Ed.), *The technology management handbook* (pp. 7-31–7-39). Boca Raton, FL: CRC Press.

Gaynor, G. H. (1990). *Achieving the competitive edge through integrated technology management*. New York: McGraw-Hill.

Gaynor, G. H. (1996). Management of technology: Description, scope, and implications. In G. H. Gaynor (Ed.), *Handbook of technology management* (pp. 1.3–1.31). New York: McGraw-Hill.

Geber, B. (1995). Does training make a difference? Prove it! *Training, 32*(3), 27–34.

Goh, S. C. (1998). Toward a learning organization: The strategic building blocks. *Advanced Management Journal, 63*(2), 15–18.

Goodman, R. A., & Lawless, M. W. (1994). *Technology and strategy: Conceptual models and diagnostics*. New York: Oxford University Press.

Governor's Commission for a Quality Workforce. (1991). *A world class vision for Wisconsin: Recommendations*. Madison: State of Wisconsin, Board of Vocational, Technical and Adult Education.

Gunderson, M., & Sharpe, A. (1998). Introduction. In M. Gunderson & A. Sharpe (Eds.), *Forging business-labour partnerships: The emergence of sector councils in Canada* (pp. 3–30). Toronto: University of Toronto Press.

Hackman, J. R., & Oldham, G. R. (1974). *The job diagnostic survey: An instrument for the diagnosis of jobs and the evaluation of job redesign projects*(Technical Report No. 4, Prepared for the Office of Naval Research and the U.S. Department of Labor Manpower Administration). New Haven, CT: Yale University.

Haddad, C. J. (1984). Technological change and reindustrialization: Implications for organized labor. In D. Kennedy (Ed.), *Labor and reindustrialization: Workers and corporate change* (pp. 137–166). University Park: Pennsylvania State University, Department of Labor Studies.

Haddad, C. J. (1987). Technology, industrialization, and the economic status of women. In B. D. Wright, M. M. Ferree, G. O. Mellow, L. H. Lewis, M.-L. D. Samper, R. Asher, & K. Claspell (Eds.). *Women, work and technology: Transformations* (pp. 33–57). Ann Arbor: University of Michigan Press.

Haddad, C. J. (1988). Technology, skill, and the education of adult workers. *Industrial Relations Research Association: Proceedings of the forty-first annual meeting*. Madison, WI: Industrial Relations Research Association.

Haddad, C. J. (1989). Labor's role in technological change: Past, present and future. In T. J. Kozik & D. G. Jansson (Eds.), *The worker in transition: Technological change* (pp. 57–62). New York: American Society of Mechanical Engineers.

Haddad, C. J. (1994). Concurrent engineering and the role of labor in product development. *Control Engineering Practice, 2*(4), 689–696.

Haddad, C. J. (1995). *Sectoral training partnerships in Canada: Building consensus through policy and practice* (Final report to the government of Canada). Ypsilanti: Eastern Michigan University, Department of Interdisciplinary Technology.

Haddad, C. J. (1996a). Operationalizing the concept of concurrent engineering: A case study from the U.S. auto industry. *IEEE Transactions on Engineering Management. 43*(2), 124–132.

Haddad, C. J. (1996b). The contribution of Canadian sectoral training councils to training strategy and practice. In Voos, P. (Ed.), *Industrial Relations Research Association: Proceedings of the forty-eighth annual meeting.* Madison, WI: Industrial Relations Research Association.

Haddad, C. J. (1996c, September). *Reengineering the organization: The role of organizational culture in simultaneous engineering.* Paper presented at the International Federation of Automatic Control (IFAC) 13th Triennial World Congress, San Francisco.

Haddad, C. J. (1996d). Employee attitudes toward new technology in a unionized manufacturing plant. *Journal of Engineering and Technology Management, 13,* 145–162.

Haddad, C. J. (1997). *Evaluation of the labor participation in modernization project: Research findings.* Unpublished report to NIST-MEP. Ypsilanti: Eastern Michigan University, Department of Interdisciplinary Technology.

Haddad, C. J. (1998). Sector councils as models of shared governance in training and adjustment. In M. Gunderson & A. Sharpe (Eds.), *Forging business-labour partnerships: The emergence of sector councils in Canada* (pp. 208–233). Toronto: University of Toronto Press.

Haddad, C. J. (2000a). Involving manufacturing employees in the early stages of product development: A case study from the U.S. automobile industry. In U. Jürgens (Ed.), *New product development and production networks: Global industrial experience* (pp. 289–312). Berlin, Germany: Springer.

Haddad, C. J. (2000b, January). *Shared governance in plant Modernization: Findings from a demonstration project in the small and medium-size firm sector.* Paper presented at the 52nd Annual Meeting of the Industrial Relations Research Association, Boston.

Hayes, K. (1998). A labour perspective on sector councils. In M. Gunderson & A. Sharpe (Eds.), *Forging business-labour partnerships: The emergence of sector councils in Canada* (pp. 61–71). Toronto: University of Toronto Press.

Hellriegel, D., Slocum, J. W., & Woodman, R. W. (1989). *Organizational behavior* (5th ed.). St. Paul, MN: West.

Herman, B. (1998). Telephone interview by C. Haddad on August 27.

Hirschhorn, L. (1984). *Beyond mechanization: Work and technology in a post-industrial age.* Cambridge: MIT Press.

Hirschhorn, L. (1989*). Training factory workers: Three case studies.* Philadelphia: Wharton Center for Applied Research.

Hirschhorn, L., Gilmore, T., & Newell, T. (1989). Training and learning in a post-industrial world. In H. Leymann & H. Kornbluh (Eds.), *Socialization and learning at work: A new approach to the learning process in the workplace and society* (pp. 185–200). Aldershot, UK: Avebury.

Howarth, C. (1984). *The way people work: Job satisfaction and the challenge of change.* Oxford, UK: Oxford University Press.

Human Resources Development Institute. (1996). Workplace change comes to Wisconsin. *HRDI Journal.* Washington, DC: Human Resources Development Institute, AFL-CIO.

Jain, H. C. (1980). *Worker participation: Success and problems.* New York: Praeger.

Jürgens, U., Malsch, T., & Dohse, K. (1993). *Breaking away from Taylorism: Changing forms of work in the automobile industry.* Cambridge, UK: Cambridge University Press.

Jurich, J. A., & Myers-Bowman, K. S. (1998). Systems theory and its application to research on human sexuality. *Journal of Sex Research, 35*(1), 72–87.

Kahn, R. L. (2000, September). *Organizational and social environments and health: Introduction.* Paper presented at ICOS seminar, 2000, University of Michigan.

Kanigel, R. (1997). *The one best way: Frederick Winslow Taylor and the enigma of efficiency.* New York: Viking.

Karlsson, U. (1995). The Swedish sociotechnical approach: Strengths and weaknesses. In J. Benders, J. de Haan, & D. Bennett (Eds.), *The symbiosis of work and technology* (pp. 47–58). London: Taylor & Francis.

King, W. R. (2001). Strategies for creating a learning organization. *Information Systems Management, 18*(1), 12–20.

Kirkpatrick, D. (1994). *Evaluating training programs: The four levels.* San Francisco: Berrett-Koehler.

Knights, D., & Murray, F. (1994). *Managers divided.* New York: John Wiley.

Kochan, T. A. (1996). Presidential address: Launching a renaissance in international industrial relations research. *Relations Industrielles—Industrial Relations, 51*(2): 247–263.

Kornbluh, H., & Greene, R. T. (1989). Learning, empowerment and participative work processes: The educative work environment. In H. Leymann & H. Kornbluh (Eds.), *Socialization and learning at work: A new approach to the learning process in the workplace and society* (pp. 256–274). Aldershot, UK: Avebury.

Kotter, J. P. (1995). Leading change: Why transformation efforts fail. *Harvard Business Review, 73*(2): 59–67.

Kusterer, K. C. (1978). *Know-how on the job: The important working knowledge of "unskilled" workers.* Boulder, CO: Westview Press.

Lambourne, K., De Pietro, R., Orta-Anes, L., & Smith, J. L. (1992). *Guidelines for implementing labor-management problem solving teams in manufacturing.* Report prepared for the Federal Mediation and Conciliation Service. Ann Arbor, MI: Industrial Technology Institute.

Latniak, E. (1995). "Technikgestaltung" (Shaping of technology) and direct participation: German experiences in managing technological change. In J. Benders, J. de Haan, & D. Bennett (Eds.), *The symbiosis of work and technology.* London: Taylor & Francis.

Leymann, H. (1989). Learning theories. In H. Leymann & H. Kornbluh (Eds.), *Socialization and learning at work: A new approach to the learning process in the workplace and society.* Aldershot, UK: Avebury.

Liker, J. K., Haddad, C. J., & Karlin, J. (1999). Perspectives on technology and work organization. *Annual Review of Sociology, 25*, 575–596.

Majchrzak, A. (1988). *The human side of factory automation: Managerial and human resource strategies for making automation succeed.* San Francisco: Jossey-Bass.

Mankin, D., Cohen, S. G., & Bikson, T. K. (1997). Teams and technology: Tensions in participatory design. *Organizational Dynamics, 26*(1), 63–76.

Manwaring, T., & Wood, S. (1984). The ghost in the machine: Tacit skills in the labour process. *Socialist Review, 3–34* (74), 55–83.

Martens, H., & Neuenfeldt, P. (1997). *Wisconsin Regional Training Partnership: Building partnerships between employers, unions & communities in the manufacturing center* (Annual report). Milwaukee: Wisconsin Regional Training Partnership.

McNabb, M., Hawkes, M., & Rouk, U. (1999, July). *Critical issues in evaluating the effectiveness of technology.* Paper presented at the U.S. Department of Education's National Conference on Educational Technology: Evaluating the Effectiveness of Technology, 1999, Washington, DC. Retrieved February 1, 2002, from www.ed.gov/Technology/TechConf/1999/confsum.html

Mikulecky, L., & Kirkley, J. R. (1998). Literacy instruction for the 21st century workplace. *Peabody Journal of Education, 73*(3–4), 290–316.

Mintzberg, H. (1994). *The rise and fall of strategic planning: Reconceiving roles for planning, plans, planners.* New York: Free Press.

Montgomery, D. (1979). *Workers' control in America: Studies in the history of work, technology and labor struggles.* Cambridge, UK: Cambridge University Press.

Morel, B., & Ramanujam, R. (1999). Through the looking glass of complexity: The dynamics of organizations as adaptive and evolving systems. *Organization Science, 10*(3), 278–293.

Morgall, J. (1993). *Technology assessment: A feminist perspective.* Philadelphia: Temple University Press.

Morse, M. (1995). *Women changing science: Voices from a field in transition.* New York: Plenum Press.

National Research Council. (1991). *People and Technology in the Workplace.* National Academy of Engineering [and] Commission on Behavioral and Social Sciences and Education, National Research Council. Washington, DC: National Academy Press.

Nissen, B. (Ed.). (1997). *Unions and workplace reorganization.* Detroit, MI: Wayne State University Press.

Noori, H. (1990). *Managing the dynamics of new technology: Issues in manufacturing management.* Englewood Cliffs, NJ: Prentice Hall.

Northcraft, G. B., & Neale, M. A. (1990). *Organizational behavior: A management challenge.* Chicago: Dryden Press.

Norton, R. E. (1992, June). *SCID: A competency-based curriculum development model.* Paper presented at the Mid-America Competency-Based Education Conference, 1992, Chicago.

Oden, H. W. (1997). *Managing corporate culture, innovation and intrapreneurship.* Westport, CT: Quorum Books.

Pacey, A. (1983). *The culture of technology.* Cambridge: MIT Press.

Parker, E., & Rogers, J. (1996). *The Wisconsin Regional Training Partnership: Lessons for national policy.* Berkeley: University of California at Berkeley, Institute of Industrial Relations.

Penn, R. (1982). Skilled manual workers in the labour process, 1856–1964. In S. Wood (Ed.), *The degradation of work? Skill, deskilling and the labour process* (pp. 90–108). London: Hutchinson.

Pipan, R. C. (1989). Towards a curricular perspective of workplaces. In H. Leymann & H. Kornbluh (Eds.), *Socialization and learning at work: A new approach to the learning process in the workplace and society* (pp. 159–180). Aldershot, UK: Avebury.

Pool, R. (1997). *Beyond engineering: How society shapes technology.* Cambridge, MA: MIT Press.

Potts, M. K., & Hagan, C. B. (2000). Going the distance: Using systems theory to design, implement, and evaluate a distance education program. *Journal of Social Work Education, 36*(1), 131–145.

Preece, D. (1995). *Organizations and technical change: Strategy, objectives and involvement.* London: Routledge.

Pursell, C. (1995). *The machine in America: A social history of technology.* Baltimore: Johns Hopkins University Press.

Reich, R. B. (1994, April). Jobs: Skills before credentials. *Training,* pp. 38–40.

Robbins, S. P. (1991). *Management* (3rd ed.). Englewood Cliffs, NJ: Prentice Hall.

Rodriguez, S. R. (1988). Needs assessment and analysis: Tools for change. *Journal of Instructional Development, 11*(1), 23–28.

Rosenbrock, H. (1990). *Machines with a purpose.* Oxford, UK: Oxford University Press.

Rosenbrock, H. H. (1983, December). Technological redundancy: Designing automated systems—Need skill be lost? *Science and Public Policy,* pp. 274–277.

Rossi, P. H., & Freeman, H. E. (1993). *Evaluation: A systematic approach* (5th ed.). Newbury Park, CA: Sage.

Roztocki, N., & Needy, K. L. (1999). Integrating activity-based costing and economic value added in manufacturing. *Engineering Management Journal, 11*(12), 17–22.

Sagie, A., & Koslowsky, M. (2000). *Participation and empowerment in organizations: Modeling, effectiveness and applications.* Thousand Oaks, CA: Sage.

Salzman, H. (1990, March). *Designing process technology for "usability": Practices and principles for strategic design of skill-based technology.* Paper presented at the Technology and the Future of Work Conference, 1990, Stanford University.

Schein, E. H. (1985). *Organizational culture and leadership.* San Francisco: Jossey-Bass.

Schilling, M. A. (2000). Toward a general modular systems theory and its application to interfirm product modularity. *Academy of Management Review, 25*(2), 312–334.

Schneider, L. (1983). *Technology bargaining in Norway.* Report prepared for the Ministry of Local Government and Labor, Oslo, Norway. Boston: Harvard Business School.

Senge, P. (1990). *The fifth discipline*. New York: Doubleday.

Shelton, S., & Alliger, G. (1993). Who's afraid of level 4 evaluation? A practical approach. *Training & Development Journal, 47*(6), 43–46.

Sitkin, S. B., Sutcliffe, K. M., & Weick, K. E. (1999). Organizational learning. In R. C. Dorf (Ed.), *The technology management handbook*. Boca Raton, FL: CRC Press.

Solomon, J. S. (1987). Union responses to technological change: Protecting the past or looking to the future? *Labor Studies Journal, 12*(2), 51–64.

Spenner, K. I. (1990). Skill: Meanings, methods, and measures. *Work and Occupations, 17*(4), 399–421.

Taylor, F. W. (1911). *The principles of scientific management*. Retrieved February 1, 2002 from www.therblig.com/taylor/title.html

Taylor, J. C. (1975). The human side of work: The socio-technical approach to work system design. *Personnel Review, 4*(3), 17–22.

Taylor, J. C., & Asadorian, R. A. (1985). The implementation of excellence: STS management. *Industrial Management, 27*(4), 5–15.

Taylor, J. C., & Felten, D. F. (1993). *Performance by design: Sociotechnical systems in North America*. Upper Saddle River, NJ: Prentice Hall.

Thompson, P., & McHugh, D. (1990). *Work organizations: A critical introduction*. London: Macmillan.

Trist, E. (1981). *The evolution of socio-technical systems: A conceptual framework and an action research program* (Occasional Paper No. 2). Toronto: Ontario Quality of Working Life Centre.

Trist, E., & Bamforth, K. W. (1951). Some social and psychological consequences of the longwall method of coal getting. *Human Relations, 4*(1), 3–38.

U.S. Congress, Office of Technology Assessment. (1990, September). *Worker training: Competing in the new international economy*, OTA-ITE-457. Washington, DC: Government Printing Office.

U.S. Department of Education. (1999). *The Secretary's Conference on Educational Technology—1999: East Detroit Public Schools, Michigan*. Retrieved February 1, 2002 from www.ed.gov/Technology/TechConf/1999/profiles/eastdetroit.html

U.S. Department of Education, National Center for Education Statistics. (1992). *1992 national adult literacy survey*. Retrieved February 1, 2002 from http://nces.ed.gov/naal/design/about92.asp

Vancouver, J. B. (1996). Living systems theory as a paradigm for organizational behavior: Understanding humans, organizations and social processes. *Behavioral Science, 41*, 165–204.

Verma, A., Lamertz, K., & Warrian, P. (1998). The Canadian Steel Trade and Employment Congress: Old-fashioned labour-management cooperation or an innovation in joint governance? In M. Gunderson & A. Sharpe (Eds.), *Forging business-labour partnerships: The emergence of sector councils in Canada*. Toronto: University of Toronto Press.

Verner, C. (1963). Basic concepts and limitations. In J. R. Kidd (Ed.), *Learning and society* (pp. 229–240). Canadian Association for Adult Education/Mutual Press Limited.

Volti, R. (1995). *Society and technological change.* New York: St. Martin's.

Wajcman, J. (1991). *Feminism confronts technology.* University Park: Pennsylvania State University Press.

Walton, R. E., Cutcher-Gershenfeld, J. E., & McKersie, R. B. (1994). *Strategic negotiations: A theory of change in labor-management relations.* Boston: Harvard Business School Press.

Webster, A. (1991). *Science, technology and society.* New Brunswick, NJ: Rutgers University Press.

Whyte, W. F. (Ed.). (1991). *Participatory action research.* Newbury Park, CA: Sage.

Witte, J. F. (1980). *Democracy, authority, and alienation in work: Workers' participation in an American corporation.* Chicago: University of Chicago Press.

Wobbe, W. (1995). Anthropocentric production systems: A new "leitbild" for an industrial symbiotic work and technology culture in Europe. In J. Benders, J. de Haan, & D. Bennett (Eds.), *The symbiosis of work and technology* (pp. 13–24). London: Taylor & Francis.

Wolfe, D. A., & Martin, D. (1998). Human resources think for themselves: The experience of unions in the sectoral skills council. In M. Gunderson & A. Sharpe (Eds.), *Forging business-labour partnerships: The emergence of sector councils in Canada.* Toronto: University of Toronto Press.

Womack, J. P., Jones, D. T., & Roos, D. (1990). *The machine that changed the world.* New York: Rawson Associates.

Zemke, R. (1999). Why organizations still aren't learning. *Training, 36*(9), 40–42.

Zemke, R., & Rossett, A. (1985). *Be a better needs analyst.* ASTD Info-Line Issue 502. Alexandria, VA: American Society for Training and Development.

Zemsky, R., & Oedel, P. (1995). Closing the gap: Private and public job training. *EQW Issues,* Number 7. Philadelphia: University of Pennsylvania, National Center on the Educational Quality of the Workforce.

Zuboff, S. (1988). *In the age of the smart machine: The future of work and power.* New York: Basic Books.

Index

About the Author

Dr. Carol Haddad is a professor in the Department of Interdisciplinary Technology at Eastern Michigan University, where she teaches graduate courses and conducts research on workplace technology and training partnerships. Her externally funded research projects have included a study of sector-based labor-management training partnerships in three Canadian industries (automotive parts, steel, and electrical/electronics); evaluation of an NIST-MEP–sponsored pilot program to expand union leader awareness of and involvement in industrial modernization; and evaluation with two other faculty members of a training program designed to promote integration of instructional technology in K-12 classroom curricula.

Dr. Haddad is also a consultant to organizations on technological change, training practices, and evaluation research. Her clients have included the IAM; IBEW and AT&T; the State of Michigan; the CWA; the UAW-Chrysler, UAW-Ford, and UAW-GM joint training centers; the Canadian Steel Trade and Employment Congress; and the USWA Canada and Algoma Steel. She lectures frequently to and conducts workshops for audiences in the United States, Canada, and Europe.

Her prior work history includes serving as a tenured faculty member in the School of Labor and Industrial Relations at Michigan State University, director of the Labor and Technology Program at the Industrial Technology Institute, senior researcher and project manager with the American Society for Training and Development, trainer for the Department of Education and Training of the American Arbitration Association, and public sector union staff member. She holds a Ph.D. from the University of Michigan and an M.S. degree from the University of Massachusetts at Amherst.